ELEGANT
Solutions

Quintessential Technology for
a User-Friendly World

ELEGANT
Solutions

by Owen Edwards

Photographs by Douglas Whyte
Design by John C Jay

CROWN PUBLISHERS, INC. NEW YORK

Copyright © 1989 by Owen Edwards

Published by Crown Publishers, Inc., 201 East 50th Street,
New York, New York 10022
CROWN is a trademark of Crown Publishers, Inc.

Manufactured in West Germany by
Universitätsdruckerei H. Stürtz AG

Layouts by Kirsti Kroener

Library of Congress Cataloging-in-Publication Data

Edwards, Owen.
Elegant solutions: quintessential technology for a user-friendly world /
by Owen Edwards; design by John Jay;
photographs by Douglas Whyte.
p.   cm.
1. Design, Industrial.   I. Title.
TS171.4.E35   1989
745.2—dc19   88-38778

ISBN 0-517-55833-5

10 9 8 7 6 5 4 3 2 1
FIRST EDITION

Parts of this book first appeared as "Quintessential Utensils" in *Cuisine* magazine, whose editor, Carey Winfrey, encouraged me to have fun but was careful not to give me enough money to get into trouble.

Several books in addition to those mentioned in the text were helpful in the search for facts and inspiration: *By Design,* by Ralph Caplan; *Eureka! An Illustrated History of Inventions from the Wheel to the Computer,* edited by Edward De Bono; *Blueprints: Twenty-six Extraordinary Structures,* by Christopher Gray and John Boswell; *The Nature of Design,* by David Pye; *A History of Architecture: Settings and Rituals,* by Spiro Kostof; *A History of the Umbrella,* by T. S. Crawford; *A Price Guide to Beer Advertising Openers and Corkscrews,* by Donald Bull; and the endlessly informative "Science" section of the *New York Times.*

I also want to thank Pam Thomas, editor and friend, who started this book off, and David Groff, who finished it up with great enthusiasm and a stern hand with egregious puns. Thanks to four other Crown jewels: Ken Sansone, Kay Riley, Amy Boorstein, and Wilson Henley, who made a book that wanted to happen into a book that has happened.

A clink of Baccarat crystal to John Jay, Bloomingdale's bloom and a designer's designer who gave style to my elements.

And a heartfelt "Cheese" to Doug Whyte, whose wonderful photographs made me see again what I thought I'd seen already.

For Betty Cornfeld,

whose talent and charm

were quintessential . . .

and for Regine,

my own elegant solution

Look at that turbine.

Nobody in America can

paint a turbine like that.

Not since the thirties.

Every part so distinct you

could rebuild one from it,

yet the whole thing

romantic as a sunset.

John Updike

Bech: A Book

If your particular problem happens to be how to get from one side of a body of water to the other, any number of well-known solutions are available. You can hold onto a floating log and hope for propitious currents. You can hollow out the log and use a branch for a paddle. You can lash logs together and build a raft. And so on up the line of technological evolution.

Let's say that you need to make the crossing regularly, without depending on the state of the tides or the mood (and greed) of a ferryman. The solution then is to build a bridge. And let's say, too, that the water to be crossed is wide and deep, and the bridge must allow clearance for ships to pass below. Given these factors, you will likely find the best solution is a suspension bridge—which, it happens, is one of the most wonderful innovations conceived by the human mind, the kind of solution that can make you grateful for the problem.

The great charm of a suspension bridge is that its grace springs inevitably from the necessities of its construction. The opposing curves of its main cables and its suspended roadway, the upward thrust of its support piers and the ranks of secondary cables reaching down—all combine to create a sculptural illusion of delicacy and weightlessness so entrancing that it almost seems to be a form of flight. The suspension bridge is one of those singularly blessed functional forms that simply cannot be ugly.

The city of San Francisco, where I now live, covers the tip of a peninsula connected to the land in the north and east by two of the finest examples of that form: the San Francisco Bay Bridge and the Golden Gate Bridge. It happens that both bridges were completed in 1937, and both were given fiftieth birthday parties not long after I arrived in the city. The Bay Bridge, as gray and looming as a San Francisco fog, was the first to be feted, in speeches and written praise for its considerable engineering achievements, and with a lavish fireworks show that accorded the handsome span a night of noisy respect.

The birthday bash for the Golden Gate Bridge, however, was an entirely different phenomenon. For only the second time in its history, the bridge was closed to cars and only pedestrian traffic was allowed. Not even the most ardent admirer of the bridge could have predicted the extraordinary response. Beginning just after dawn on the twenty-fourth of May, lines of walkers began winding up the hills toward the bridge from the north and south. By midmorning, the gathering of celebrants was estimated to be more than six hundred thousand, equaling the population of San Francisco itself. Had it not been for television helicopters and buzzing flocks of antique airplanes, the scene would have seemed almost medieval; this was not simply a holiday celebration, it was a mass gathering of pilgrims at a shrine. Pictures taken that day reveal that the crowd was so dense the arc of the center span actually flattened. Though at the time I was a newcomer to the city, the bridge had already exerted its effect on me, and I was in the midst of the devoted throng, unable to take a step in any direction for most of the morning. Yet despite the crush, everyone seemed to be in high spirits and nobody was in a hurry to be anywhere but there on the bridge. The party went on long into the night, with the bay so thick with the lights from boats assembled to watch the fireworks that it looked like a city itself. If respect and admiration characterized the celebration of the Bay Bridge, the birthday of the Golden Gate was memorable for a vast outpouring of something very close to love.

What made the difference? Both structures are estimable works of technology, and both have the innate beauty of suspension bridge design. But the Golden Gate Bridge represents a further achievement, a milestone in the realm of art. Irving Morrow, the architect who created the bravura style of the bridge (a man with such a radical reputation he had never been commissioned to design a major building), understood that the extraordinary setting of the entrance to San Francisco Bay deserved architecture no less splendid. Working with a graceful basic structure drawn up by an engineer named Charles A. Ellis—the original plan by chief engineer Joseph B. Strauss was a top-heavy monstrosity —Morrow calculated every detail to appeal to the eye and the heart. The pylons were designed like skyscrapers, with setbacks that narrow their towering forms as they rise and a geometric motif of vertical facets and art deco embellishments to unify the various elements and draw the eye upward. Morrow also kept the X braces typical of steel pylons below the roadway and sheathed the cross braces above to simplify the bridge's lines. From lighting fixtures to railings, Morrow left nothing out of his grand design and in the end created a work on a par with the greatest architecture of this century. Arching gracefully from one shore to the other, the dramatic red bridge stands as an ultimate solution to an ancient problem. But with its power to arouse the emotions of the humans who cross it, the span is something much more: it is an elegant solution.

In mathematics and physics, the term *elegant solution* indicates a way of solving a problem that is correct and efficient, but beyond that is also pleasing to contemplate. In his book *The Discoverers,* Daniel Boorstin recounts that Copernicus, in searching for an alternative to the Ptolemaic planetary system (which seemed to fit observed appearances), was motivated by his desire to find an explanation for the movement of the planets that "would not merely satisfy the eye [but] would also . . . please the mind." In other words, the astronomer felt that such a cosmic question deserved an elegant solution.

On a more earthbound level, an elegant solution is a way to solve a practical problem well, but to do so with an unexplainable quality that might as well be called charisma. An elegant solution accomplishes its task in what we know instinctively is the most admirable way (whether or not it is demonstrably the best). When San Franciscans see the Golden Gate Bridge, or New Yorkers gaze up at the Chrysler Building or the Empire State, a feeling of gratitude rises up for a thing that gives form so eloquently to humanity's aspirations and ingenuity. On a less grand but no less meaningful plane, a similar feeling can be aroused by a wonderfully designed car, a well-formed pen, a fine hammer, or a nonpareil piece of clothing.

Although there is no specific guide for identifying an elegant solution, no precise checklist useful in judging a telephone or a toothbrush, one's instinctive reaction is usually a trustworthy measure. Mythologist Joseph Campbell spoke often about the decisive moment when one looks at a "fortunately composed work of art and says 'Aha!' " Much the same thing happens when you come upon an elegant solution. Describing the qualities of architect Otto Wagner's houses, critic John Russell wrote of "comfort, amenity, distinction of mind, and an evident rightness of proportion." He might have been writing about any one of the things that appear in this book. The operative word is *evident*. Something within us loves an elegant solution and recognizes one on sight.

Whether we admit it or not, we are all machine-age animists, convinced that manufactured things are inhabited by spirits that we can negotiate with, entreat, or coerce. So we mutter threats at our coffee machines, worry about the workload of our computers, and suspect our cars run better after we've lovingly washed and waxed them. Just as primitive tribes sought to propitiate the souls of trees and rivers, we hope to forge alliances with the things we use every day, believing our intercession can make them—in the entirely apt current terminology—user friendly. John Updike summed up this modern animism in his novel *Of The Farm* when he described the "absolute tenderness" of a tractor, and the sensation of driving one as "enthronement atop a great obligingness." With similar feeling, a bomber pilot once wrote of his plane: "After a while, you develop a relationship to a machine, you understand it, and you think that it understands you." With elegant solutions, as with cars, computers, tractors, and B-29's, a sense of mutual understanding is the heart of the matter.

In the relentless, never-ending game of Darwinners and losers, problem solving is humanity's trump card. Ever since the first overachieving primate used a stick to knock fruit from a tree (or intimidate a fellow primate interested in the same fruit), we have evolved as we have solved. Somewhere along the way, we elevated the act of solving problems to a holy quest (and made saints of our Newtons, Einsteins, Oppenheimers, and Cricks) until it seems entirely sane and eminently moral to think up exotic problems—tracking down the charmed quark, for instance—simply to find ways to solve them. Whether the problem or its solution are felicitous or even useful are points often lost in the process. Not having to figure out how to get fruit out of trees anymore, we strive to breed square fruit for more profitable packing.

Our obsessive problem solving itself poses a problem. Compulsively, we think up new solutions to problems that have been nicely solved already. We can't leave well enough alone, but convince ourselves that the very concept "well enough" is an enemy of progress and banish it from our thoughts. We ignore the wisdom of King Lear, who warned that "striving to better, oft we mar what's well," or the sensible advice of hardscrabble Alabama farmers, who advise not to fix "what ain't broke."

A substantial amount of change is built into our economic system, and, of course, the competition of free enterprise plays a key role in technological evolution. The trouble is that change tends to imply progress whether or not it *is* progress. Once, you had to build a better mousetrap to succeed, but now you can build an entirely ordinary mousetrap and simply convince the world that it's better because it's different. Economic incentives for change encourage a constant flow of *faux* improvements that make it harder to know the real thing when it comes along. For instance, in 1987, when General Motors executives at last realized the company had lost its traditional dominance of the American car market, they arranged a lavish show of experimental prototypes to give the impression that GM was riding the wave of the future. (The show itself was an old fifties ploy revived.) One of the fantasy vehicles substituted an airplane-style control stick for the traditional steering wheel. That idea alone was enough to make anyone buy Ford stock. For more than eight decades, the steering wheel has done its job exceptionally well, not only as a practical device allowing a driver maximum control, but as a symbolic shape, the guiding wheel within the wheels. Though it can be made smaller, or thicker, or collapsible in case of a collision, the steering wheel cannot be replaced to any good end; the notion to do so, however theoretical, is so wrongheaded that it borders on the criminally inane.

Why should we care if a thousand new, unimproved mousetraps spring into being, or if GM wants to introduce a car that plays at being a fighter plane? Because every new solution, and each revision to existing solutions, presents a potential risk. If it is valid, progress *is* progress, but if it is specious, real harm is done. A form of Gresham's law operates that causes bad ideas and bad products to crowd out good ones by debasing the currency of design itself.

Each year in the United States, some sixty-six thousand patents are granted. In all over the years, more than four and a half million have been issued. Many of the inventions among these patents never get beyond the planning stage, most have little effect on our lives, and the great majority have only the briefest lives themselves. But many actually do become products. A few are miraculous, like the laser "scalpel" that has revolutionized eye surgery, and many are egregious, like the electric bug zapper. Most are neither necessary nor capable of inspiring more than passing desire. And as they appear, make their run at success, and vanish unmourned, discontent builds up within those of us who feel that the things we buy and use have a metaphoric significance. Just as a great bridge can engender the feeling that all is well (or could be well if only everything were so well conceived), a badly designed telephone can make us suspect, every time we pick it up, that life is sliding downhill.

No matter how dazzling a piece of technology may be, the way we feel about it creature-to-creature—its ability to reassure our inner animist—can never be discounted. The late Philip Estridge, who headed up IBM's personal computer division, once observed that "the most important thing we learned was that how people reacted to a personal computer emotionally was almost more important than what they did with it."

In a world ever more crowded with products that heighten our anxieties through disappointment, suspicion, anger, and resentment, where shoddiness of design and manufacture seem to endow things with malign spirits that first enthrall and then bedevil us, where the once-hopeful word *technology* has taken on a reverberation of dread, an elegant solution is a reminder that the well-tempered device remains decidedly possible. It exists in a material state of grace that is nothing short of revelatory to those who recognize it.

espite the frenetic clutter of high dreck surrounding us, elegant solutions aren't at all hard to find. They are at hand, often fulfilling the most ordinary functions. Spaghetti, eyeglasses, the button, and the ball bearing all qualify. The inclined plane is elegant, as is its homiest application, the wood screw. The staircase is elegant, though not quite as elegant as its aristocratic cousin, the spiral staircase. No matter how extraordinary an elegant solution may be, and how great its obligingness, it's as likely to be common as rare. In *The Periodic Tables,* Primo Levi wrote that "true beauty, in which every century recognizes itself, is found in upright stones, ships' hulls, the blade of an ax, the wing of a plane." To this list can be added such simple perfections as the golf ball, shoe trees, the umbrella, and the safety razor. An elegant solution, plainly defined, is something pleasing to see (if you bother to stop and look), pleasing to use, and, not least, pleasing to contemplate, like the solar system according to Copernicus. An elegant solution is a true working-class hero.

Aside from nature's creations, there are no perfect solutions. Everything humanity concocts comes with some cost attached. Solutions that seem flawless at first may have repercussions no one ever anticipated; witness the nuclear golem that rose up out of Einstein's impeccable $E = mc^2$, or the glaciers of eternal trash spawned by the miracle of plastic. Effects ripple out from innovation in imponderable ways. Clive Sinclair, the English electronics wizard, has said that you can't be a good inventor without considering the kind of world you want to live in. Yet even if due consideration is given, there are no guarantees that a good idea won't end up causing havoc. The Gnostics believed that every human action, whether trivial or grand, incorporates both good and evil, and the best one can do is try to favor the good.

Elegant solutions, by adding emotional benefits to their practical ingenuity, pay back more than any price they may exact. Producing psychic gain while mitigating the inevitable pain of progress, they offer an abundance of what theologian Jean Le Moyne called "the charity of the machine." In a most fundamental way, the number of elegant solutions available to a society is a measure of that society's well-being.

Inept solutions (or merely expedient ones), nondurable goods, and opportunistic concepts all reveal a kind of entropy, one that little by little erodes our faith in the future, and in ourselves. If, as architectural historian Spiro Kostof writes, "Design is the graph of attitude," then an ill-conceived car or a badly realized chair are more than annoyances; they are saboteurs of the soul. Elegant solutions are the best defense.

On the following pages, I offer a random sampling of elegant solutions, ranging from such common marvels as the paper clip and Q-tips to formidable dream machines like the Concorde SST and the Porsche 911SC. I've made no attempt to be definitive or all-inclusive, but hope simply to indicate what an elegant solution is; in effect, to remind readers what they know already by paying homage to the admirable qualities of often-seen objects. The things chosen represent the arbitrariness of a compulsive list maker's art, with no categories and no hierarchy. Some are the end product of highly sophisticated design concepts, and some are simply the inevitable forms demanded by their functions. Most of the objects in this book are industrial designs, though there are also items of clothing, jewelry, a notable example of graphic design (the "tails" side of the dollar bill), and one venerable patent medicine.

Since elegant solutions are far more important as part of life than as displays in a museum, my intent is to celebrate things that are currently available. Unfortunately, the whims of the marketplace and the rigors of business are not necessarily respecters of good design (the word *new* having an attraction for manufacturers often fatal to worthy products). Some of my choices, therefore, may already be marked for oblivion, and some will be changed from the way they appear here. But the concept of the elegant solution is what matters, not how current a catalogue of examples should be, and the things in this book are meant to illustrate that concept with their worthiness and wit.

Most important, though elegant solutions by definition do well what they are intended to do, it's possible that other things do the same job better.

The sizzle of our technological age is in superlatives —products are touted for their speed, their stylishness, their gee-whiz complexity, the number of tasks they can perform at the touch of a button. But the beauty of an elegant solution is only partly functional, and only partly aesthetic; a further, unseen but instantly recognizable dimension of rightness—the "Aha!" factor—lifts them above any competition for statistical superiority. A hundred arguments can be made, for instance, against the inclusion of the Concorde jetliner in a book of successful designs, since in many ways the plane isn't a success at all. It's noisy, economically unrewarding, fuel inefficient, ecologically questionable, rather small inside, and no longer in production. Yet to see the Concorde lifting majestically off a runway is to recapture ancient dreams of flight that have long been buried under the tedium of commuting at thirty thousand feet.

Everything in this book will satisfy a practical need, but what really matters is that each will satisfy a deeper yearning, a need for things to be admirable and intelligent, generous and sound, functional and spiritual. For after all the measurements are made and all the sales pitches completed, elegant solutions stand out because they are truly objects of our affection.

Owen Edwards

*Do you believe in money? Don't pro-*test that it's the root of all evil, that it can't buy happiness, that you really never think about it. Do you believe in it? Of course you do. We all do—whether or not money believes in us. And deep down in the safe-deposit boxes of our souls, the money we believe in is the U.S. dollar, a.k.a. the Federal Reserve note, the greenback, the almighty buck. Never mind that it's not quite what it used to be; in this we trust.

*W*hy is that? After all, paper money has an intrinsic value of nothing; its worth depends on a very large number of people tacitly agreeing to go along with the illusion that it *is* worth something. For money to retain this chimerical value, all sorts of factors come into play, including a stable economy, a reasonably controlled balance of payments, and more than a little cock-eyed optimism. But though Adam Smith and John Maynard Keynes inexplicably failed to mention it, one factor must certainly be the power of the currency itself to inspire confidence. In this respect, be it petro-, Euro-, or just plain homegrown cabbage, the dollar is the real thing.

*M*aybe the credit for this should go to George Washing-ton, whose portrait, engraved from a Gilbert Stuart original, has such an avuncular honesty about it. But the dollar's flip side—surely one of the zaniest public designs ever produced—deserves credit too rarely given. Its odd mix of magic and monumentality seems to satisfy the deepest needs of our anxious inner exchequers.

*S*urprisingly, the dollar we know and love hasn't been around all that long. Not until 1928 was there such a thing as a standardized bill. Before that the size was larger, like its worth. And any given denomination might have a variety of graphic designs (giving rise, perhaps, to the saying, "Another day, another dollar"). The back of the dollar in its present madcap form came along in 1935, and if it looks like something created by a committee, it was. Edward H. Weeks was the project head for the Bureau of Engraving. The prosperous looking letters and numbers were the work of one G. Rose. The web-like background engraving (complete with a few hidden spiders) was done by J. Eissler (though it might as well have been Escher). And the Great Seal, the stamp that makes all government documents official, with its staring pyramid (a Masonic symbol dear to the hearts of several founding fathers) and testy eagle, was designed in 1906 by R. Ponichau. Happily for all connoisseurs of art and commerce, the buck stopped there.

Gem
PAPER CLIP

If all that survives of our fatally flawed civilization is the humble paper clip, archaeologists from some galaxy far, far away may give us more credit than we deserve. In our vast catalog of material innovation, no more perfectly conceived object exists. To watch a Middle Eastern bank teller bind together bank notes with a straight pin (a practice dating back to early Roman times) is to comprehend the paper clip's amazing grace.

*W*ith its bravura loop-within-a-loop design, the clip corrals the most chaotic paper simply by obeying Hooke's law: A body when stretched will tend to resume its original shape. No less important, paper clips provide the single most accessible supply of handy wire for a thousand tasks facing office-bound humanity. The relentlessly inquisitive Germans initiated a study that found only one out of five paper clips is ever used to bind papers, as if we clip abusers needed to be told.

*T*hough a Norwegian named Johann Vaaler is sometimes credited with inventing the clever clip in 1899, versions of it may have appeared as early as the 1870s. The first mass manufacturer was Gem Limited, of England, and Gem, whose nicely named Tuffy is pictured here in various states of distress, still manufactures the majority of the twenty billion or so clips made each year. Most of these are used and discarded, or, like their users, sometimes bent out of shape. But when willfully misused, paper clips have new and ingenious uses, from cleaning lint out of typewriters to forming chains of worry beads for vexed execs. Let's hope at least one, in mint condition, survives to tell our tale.

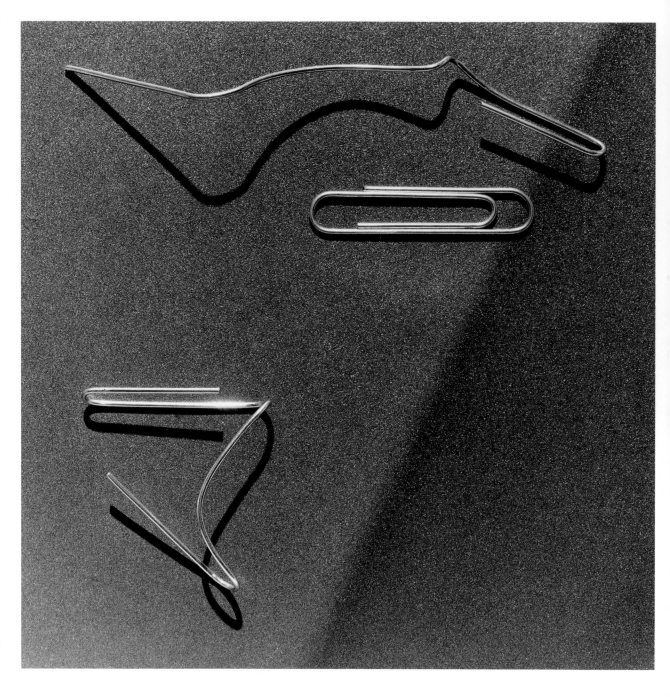

From the sublime to the ridiculous, all things are just arrangements of molecules. Who can explain why certain arrangements give us pleasure and others don't? To wit: the best champagne served in an ordinary glass won't taste as good as it should. Ridiculous. Illogical. Nonsensical and unscientific. How can it be? Maybe it's because molecules are awful snobs, and style keeps company most happily with style. Whatever, the indubitably right glass for the class drink is the Baccarat flute. Its gently flaring shape retains the effervescence yet doesn't block access even to someone whose nose is less delicate than the wine's. The exquisite joining of glass and stem is one of industrial design's most alluring details. In the best of Baccarat, the likes of Dom and Cristal find their molecular match. What better way to celebrate life's triumphs than with a twenty-one-flute salute?

Baccarat

C H A M P A G N E   F L U T E

*If, as the saying goes, architecture is fro*zen music (much of it, alas, rather bad music), then it follows that music must be thawed architecture. And it follows further that good music ought to be reproduced from machines whose architecture lives up to the great edifices of Bach, Mozart, Mendelssohn, and Monk. But most stereos resemble the dashboard of a 1953 Buick or the instrument panel on a Boeing 747; with their digital readouts, endless ranks of knobs and switches, and restless blinking lights—what some have called "Tokyo by night"— the typical components draw more attention to themselves than to the music.

*T*o solve the problem of making a truly architectural stereo, the Analog & Digital Systems Company, in Wilmington, Massachusetts, hired Dieter Rams, the German designer who put the Braun calculator on the aesthetic map. By making each component exactly the same size and shape, Rams created a look of monolithic power, harmonious and just a bit ominous. This effect is enhanced by a matte black high-impact plastic with a surface resembling slate; the stacked components would look right at home at Stonehenge. Rams has a way with buttons, and the controls on the ADS feel substantial, not disembodied in the untactile manner of modern electronic appliances. In a technology as changeable as tie widths, the ADS Atelier system has the rare character of the best music *and* the best architecture, destined to go from ahead of its time to classic without stopping at passé.

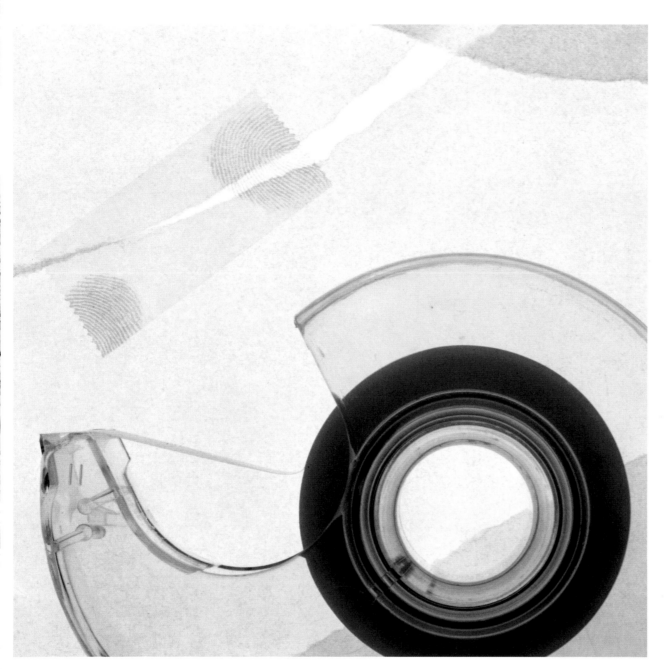

*I*f you
think the name has anything
to do with natty plaid packaging or
Highlands ingenuity, think again. In
1925, when Richard Drew, a young
correspondence-school engineer working
as a technician for the 3M Company—a
maker of sandpaper—delivered the first
batch of an adhesive masking tape he
had developed for a car painter, the experimental stuff fell off halfway through
the job. To save development costs on
the new tape, the earnest inventor had
put glue only at the outer edges of the
tape, and the painter angrily told Drew
that he could take his tape back to his
cheapskate "Scotch" bosses. The name
stuck, even if the tape didn't.

*B*y 1930, the sticky
problem of adhesion was solved, and
Drew had developed a decorated cellophane tape for packing bakery goods.
The tape business was thus launched
with annual sales of thirty-three dollars.
In its report to stockholders that year,
3M ventured the cautious view that the
packaging market "appears to have large
possibilities."

*T*hough Richard
Drew was the inventor of the tape itself,
credit for customer sanity belongs to
John A. Borden, who designed the first
heavy-duty dispenser and saved those
lost souls chronically unable to find the
cut end of the tape.

*T*o gauge Scotch
tape's importance, try imagining life
without it. Consider, for instance, what a
bad wrap Christmas would get. Or just
how you'd manage to put together your
torn thousand-dollar bills. Or, worst of
all, how you'd get the lint off your navy
blue blazer.

Swatch

*W*e may *not understand time, but we* want to believe that at the heart of its mystery there's something familiar, like a moving stream or some vast set of gears and cosmic ticktocks. Which is why the most beautiful device for measuring the minutes is the hourglass, a three-dimensional infinity sign carrying the sands of time in the flesh (as it were). At the other end of the aesthetic scale is the dismal digital watch, that forced march of enslaved electrons. Even the most style conscious among us will balk at wearing an hourglass on the wrist, but the transparent Swatch is a thoroughly satisfying alternative. The Swatch, which derives its name by compressing *Swiss watch* and has done its share to revitalize Switzerland's clockwork reputation, has a circular face (analog, if you prefer), thus honoring the brilliantly metaphoric dial invented by Jacopo de Dondi in 1344. Unlike the damnable digital, the Swatch reveals that time has a past and a future as well as a present. But most important, the Swatch has guts, and you can see them, a reminder that the workings of time are real.

*T*hough it may be true that time is measured by the decaying of protons at the far edge of the Big Bang's memory, and not by toothed gears and transistors like those that inhabit the clear shell of the Swatch, seeing what makes things tick—even though hardly anything actually moves in the Swatch's quartz innards—somehow makes comprehensible (if not enjoyable) the uncoilings of mortality.

*Q*uite a *lot of limp rhapsodizing goes* on about the creative process. We are meant to imagine the whole business as a sequence of romantic gestures—graceful hands dramatically placed on furrowed brows, eyes searching the horizon, fingers dancing on typewriter keys as the inspired one leans forward intently at the urging of his muse. Left out of this poetry of motions is that invaluable but unromantic commonplace, the fidget.

*W*ithout the fidget, nothing creative would ever get done. For that matter, nothing would get done that demanded the act of sitting down and *doing* it. Whenever our minds are at work, our bodies—temporarily vestigial—get a sudden urge to play. Fidgeting is the pressure valve of a jumpy species controlled by an organ—the brain—whose idea of physical activity is to lie there imagining push-ups.

*T*he trouble with most of the chairs on which we sit while trying to work is that they don't even pay hip service to the fidget. Like martinet math teachers, such chairs admonish us rigidly to *sit still!* What they ought to be doing, however, is letting us twitch and squirm all we want so we won't constantly jump up and stalk profitlessly around the room wishing we had become big league shortstops.

*T*he equable Equa, designed by Bill Stumpf and Don Chadwick and a platoon of innovative engineers at the Herman Miller Company in Zeeland, Michigan, is a rare chair that places the fidget on a par with the bright idea. Introduced in 1984 after more than six years of development, the Equa is as good as a chair can get in nearly every way. But its two most significant advances are in the injection-molded seat and the front-hinged tilt mechanism, which allow the sitter to squirm freely without ending up at the chiropractor, and to lean far back with feet still planted firmly on the ground.

*L*ike the best sort of muse, the Equa is supportive and giving. When it arrives, about 80 percent of the excuses for neglecting work vanish (which may or may not be a welcome change). The leather-covered top-end version of the Equa shown here weighs in at over a thousand dollars, very pricey as these things go. But for a work of art that actually works for you, why sit still for anything less?

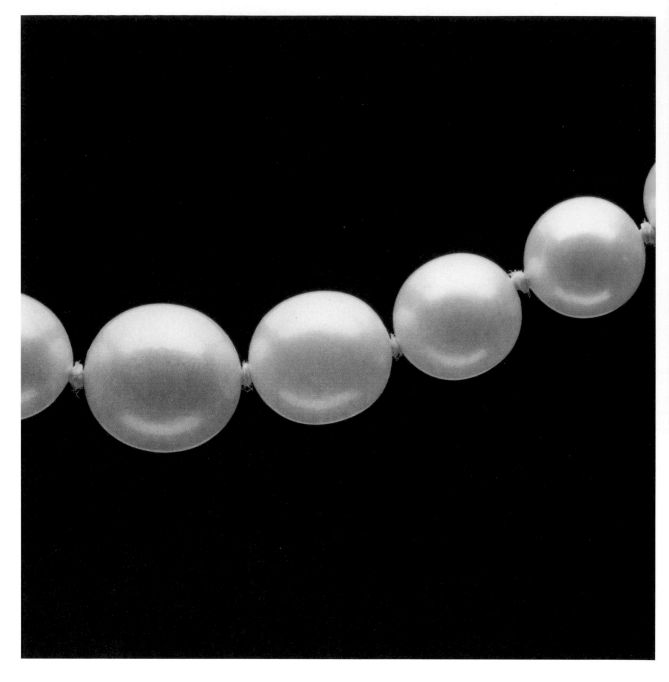

Diamonds as big as the Ritz can make the stateliest beauty look like a chandelier, and ropes of rubies evoke Victorian parlor lamps. But the single strand of pearls is neither showy nor diffident, merely unforgettable; pure, impeccable, invariably just right, a masterwork of the bivalve's art. Manufactured by the same labor-intensive process for the past million or so years—the gradual building up of nacreous layers over an irritating grain of sand—pearls are a glowing reminder that it really is possible to make the best of an uncomfortable situation. They are the romantic medal of honor for the infinitely desirable women who move hauntingly across the country club dance floors of youth and into the pages of Fitzgerald, O'Hara, and Cheever.

*T*he wonder of a single strand of perfectly matched pearls is simplicity itself: whether a woman is happy or sad, serene or distressed, her pearls form a sweet smile, either to echo the allure of her own, or to serve as a shimmering substitute until the real thing comes along.

*A*mong
the many virtues of Pears soap
is that it's not made from pears. Or avo-
cados or cold cream. Pears is a proper
soap bearing a proper name, that of
A & F Pears, of London. It contains only
a soupçon of oils (or is it soapçon?) and
glycerin, a civilized ingredient also useful in the fabrication of dynamite. A bar
of Pears, after a couple days' use, feels as
good and friendly as a fresh egg. And if
there is anything that exactly defines the
smell of soap—or at least what true soap
ought to smell like—it is Pears, with its
discreet bouquet of rosemary, thyme,
and cedar. It also displays the rare virtue
of getting better and better as it gets
older, growing more delicate and transparent as it grows smaller.

     *T*hough Pears soap
has been around for almost two hundred
years, its package doesn't insist on tell-
ing you its story, like certain other soaps
that shall remain unnamed (and un-
praised). Quietly, with admirable British
restraint, the Pears box simply displays
the squeaky clean escutcheons of Queen
Elizabeth and the Queen Mum. Which
seems quite appropriate, since those two
get better as they get older, too.

Pears

T R A N S P A R E N T   S O A P

GNT Danmark

Everybody talks on the telephone, but nobody does anything about it. Philosophically speaking, that is. At the very least, we could admit that for all its proliferation—into hotel bathrooms and cars and attaché cases and our sex lives—and all its financial success, the phone is a failed technology. After all, Mr. Bell's original idea was to help us communicate, but do we? At best, the merest edges of ideas—enough demifacts to tell us where to be, at what time, and so forth—can be transmitted through the phone's resistant lines. But more than that has proved elusive. We reach out, but we rarely manage to touch someone.

*A*s a design problem, the telephone has not been much of a success, either, spawning such objects as the Kermit the Frog phone and the pathetic Princess. Over the years, the best phones have been what AT&T calls "the basic black instrument." Like the little black dress and the tuxedo, this standard model had a certain austere dignity about it, the unobtrusive presence of a good butler. The best of these phones were designed in the thirties by Henry Dreyfus; they weighed a portentous ton, and their sculpted handsets were a joy to hold. But as time passed, the basic black became shinier and less substantial until it lost much of its elemental appeal.

*I*n a modern and appropriately minimal way, the GNT Danmark telephone has brought back the subtle luxe of a time when Nick Charles used to ring up Nora with the urgent appeal to mix up the martinis. Designed by Henning Andreassen, the sleek Danmark weighs less than two pounds, yet has a visual heft that implies

the possibility of conversational gravity.

Thoroughly modern, the phone has nothing so quaint as a bell, just a selection of odd electronic trills. And with no letters on its number buttons, the final knell has rung for such glorious vestiges as Butterfield 8 and Plaza 9. But hello and good-bye to all that; the Danmark has a phonelike look just right for communicationlike communications.

*T*hanks for calling, Watson . . . let's do lunch soon.

The beauty of the soft-boiled egg is that it provides its own container, and the triumph of the eggcup is that it serves that graceful and unimprovable container with such humility, duplicating half of the ovoid shape, then inverting it to form a stand (the whole thing ending up as a porcelain palindrome). Though the eggcup alone has its own beauty, it becomes complete only when performing its primary function. Despite this, the cup is no single-use item, like the snail plate or the lobster fork. It makes a handsome salt bowl, far more commodious than those itsy-bitsy bits of crystal that are too small to find in a pinch, and can double as a dish for soy sauce when the cuisine is Oriental but the accoutrements aren't.

A good argument can be made that the most satisfying designs are anthropomorphic, like the chair, or the front end of a '59 Cadillac. With its corsetted waist, plump bosom, and full skirt, the eggcup looks reassuringly like some doting aunt, waiting patiently but firmly to make sure you've eaten enough breakfast. No small comfort, at just the time of day when we need it most.

Fisher

The ballpoint pen, perfect emblem of the unbeautiful efficiency of the postwar world, is a marvel without substance. Much of what we write with it exerts a force as close to zero gravity as anything we're likely to encounter on earth— grocery lists, losing lottery numbers, insincere thank-you cards for the 100 percent-acrylic aqua Christmas socks, indecipherable notes for semiotics courses, and so forth. For this reason, no more apt ballpoint exists than the Space Pen, made by the Fisher Pen Company, of Forest Park, Illinois, a stylish little stylus meant to be used in the weightlessness of space. Among the pen's attributes are a streamlined shape that looks about right for attaining orbit, and the ability to write at temperatures ranging from –50°F to 400°F (for those who live in Chicago). The Space Pen also writes underwater and over grease, should such behavior be called for, and will dutifully await your pleasure for a hundred years without drying up, which is more than you can do for it. All this is made possible by a tungsten carbide ball, and thixotropic ink (a gel that liquefies when shaken and hardens when at rest) kept under fifty pounds per square inch of pressure by a stiff shot of nitrogen. The Space Pen has been used by astronauts and cosmonauts alike, making it the write stuff for the *glasnost* era. Of course, it may be argued that a piece of equipment designed for the hard life beyond the stratosphere is redundant on easy-street Earth, but it's nice to know that a lowly ballpoint has reached so high. As a spin-off of the space program, it's light years ahead of Tang.

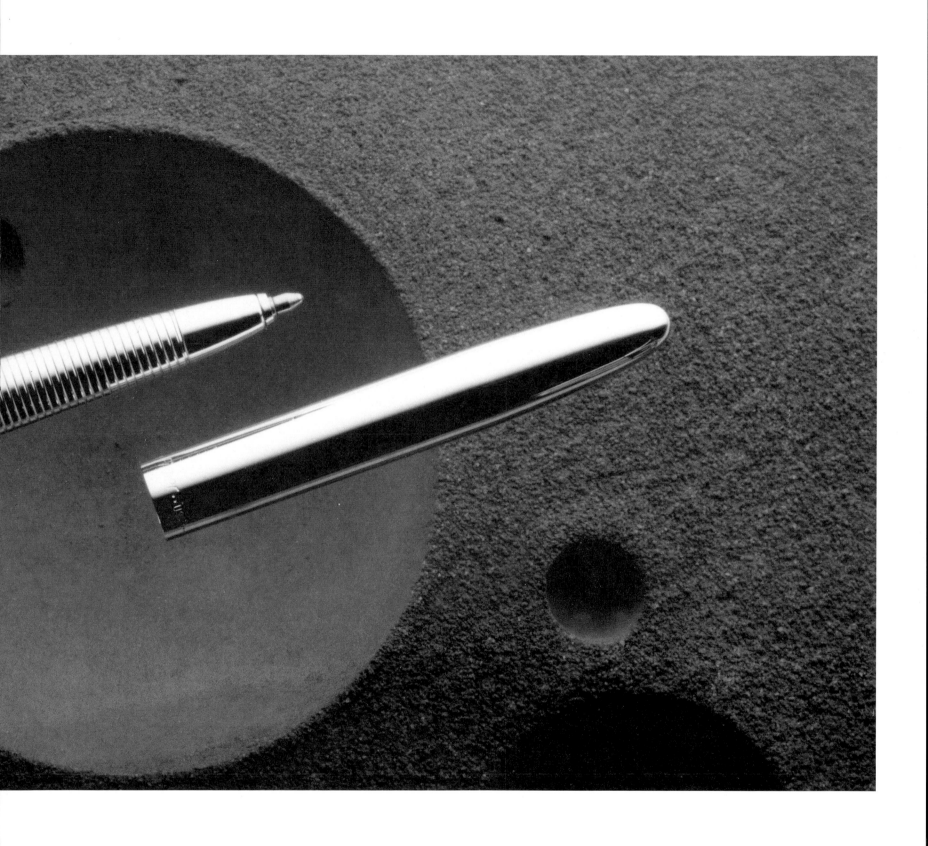

Talon

Back in the days of unemancipated sex, just getting undressed was a commitment. Clothes were secured by regimental arrangements of buttons and bows, hooks and eyes, decorative pins and doodads, all so fiercely resistant to feverish fingers that not even the most casual dalliance could be taken lightly.

Life and love proceeded at the stately pace dictated by the laborious undoings of greatcoats and smallclothes. Thus, the inventive impulse that produced the zipper may have been driven as urgently by the libido as by the intellect.

*T*he zipper was an idea whose time was a long while coming. In the early 1890s, a Chicago engineer named Whitcomb L. Judson happened to show his drawings for a shoe "clasp locker and unlocker" to Colonel Lewis Walker (colonel as in Colonel Sanders), an entrepreneur who knew a breakthrough when he saw one. Walker bought the invention, founded the Universal Fastener Company (which became Talon in 1937), and began a series of ill-fated attempts to perfect and market Judson's prescient idea.

*T*hrough many years, many failures (including the decidedly unsecure C-Curity fastener), and a few fortunes, the colonel kept the faith. In 1906, he hired an engineer named Gideon Sundback, whose improvements eventually launched the zipper age in 1913 with the inauspiciously named Hookless No. 2. Though the term *zip* appeared around 1905 in an advertising illustration, the word *zipper* may not have been officially coined until 1923, when the faster fastener appeared on B. F. Goodrich galoshes.

*C*learly, galoshes do not a libido satisfy. The revolutionary device might have languished if designer Elsa Schiaparelli hadn't found it simply *too* amusing and, in 1930, changed the nature, or at least the speed, of the romantic liaison by including a back zipper on one of her dress designs (with a single hook at the top for one last moment to reconsider the whole thing).

*T*he modern Talon is so finely machined that it's more a whisper than a zipper, but it still has the fun-house magic of its ancestors: two different sides go in one door unattached and come out the other brilliantly married. All that really goes on in there is that the slider spreads one set of teeth to let the others fit between them. Simple, but certainly no snap.

*Ironically, the more sophisticated real air-*planes get, the more they look like the basic paper model. In its happy simplicity, the paper airplane *is* flight, sleeker than the F-16 and unimaginably cheaper. *N*o one knows who made the first of these Ur-craft, but there can be little doubt that the invention preceded Wilbur and Orville by a considerable span of time. It's not hard to imagine that pioneer flight theoretician Leonardo fabricating parchment gliders to while away the empty hours (if he ever *had* any empty hours). No one knows how many variations on the theme there are, either, but when *Scientific American* held a paper airplane contest in 1967, more than twelve thousand designs were submitted, and the winner flew over fifty-eight feet. The standard model, pictured here belly-up, has a tendency to stall, but never mind—it's as satisfying an aerodynamic shape as any ever invented. Stewardess, another piece of paper, please.

P A P E R   A I R P L A N E

en's shoes tend to behave themselves in public, but when on their own in the closet they get all sorts of self-indulgent ideas. The most common is an unseemly Turkish-style curling-up-at-the-toe trick. The best way to control these wanton creatures is to fool them with surrogate feet. Since hiring others to stand in our closets is impractical, expensive, and probably immoral, the appropriate answer is the wooden shoe tree, like these best-in-breed entries carved out of aromatic cedar by the Rochester Shoe Tree Company, of Ashland, New Hampshire.

*T*he shoe tree came into being—probably in late-eighteenth-century England—as the boot tree, a trunkish form that insured decorum in the footwear of landed gentry who expected their bespoke riding boots to last considerably longer than themselves. Originally, carved boot and shoe trees were modeled after the feet of the buyer, but our more democratic and pedestrian age has brought forth a spring-loaded, segmented style that provides a custom fit for you and a vast number of like-minded (though different-footed) fellow citizens. Whether shaping up luxuries from Lobb or imposing an iron will on basics from Bass, the shoe tree is the surest sign of a cultured closet where good form starts from the ground up.

The first recorded use of lenses to cor- rect sight came sometime late in the thirteenth century, somewhat before the invention of designer frames and contacts that turn brown eyes blue.

*T*he simplest use of the lens, and probably one of the most ancient, is the magnifying glass, a single lens put on a handle, like this perfectly balanced version made by Bausch & Lomb. Hold it between your eye and a printed page—this printed page, for instance—anD MAGICALLY EVERY-THING GROws, just like Alice post-mushroom. A surprising discovery of the magnifying glass is that almost everything (except, perhaps, one's bloodshot eye) looks more interesting bigger. The feeling of astonishment at seeing things you've never suspected is one of the better cheap thrills around. And, as a fine dividend, you can use one of these lenses to focus the sun's rays on a crinkled autumn leaf and partake in the power of Prometheus without paying the price.

*I*n the last, Las Vegas days of his life, Howard Hughes had to use a magnifying glass in order to read. He called the device his "peepstone," a brilliantly odd term that by itself would have justified including the glass in this book of meaningful manufactured metaphors.

Bausch & Lomb

M A G N I F Y I N G   G L A S S

If ever there was an art form of the people, by the people, and for the people, it is the Great American Snapshot, thanks be to George Eastman and his hard working Brownies. May it never fade.

*M*ysteriously, though the snapshot may be a mere trifle to take, it can end up being the repository of family history, an icon of numinous power that will let Granddad and his lodge brothers live on long after all who ever knew them are gone. Thus, the metaphorically perfect snapshot camera should combine technical ease with a feeling of solid substantiality. The early Kodaks did just that, with their boxy, no-frills bulk. And the very model of a modern inheritor of the snapshot mystique is the handsome Olympus XA, made by Olympus Optical Company, of Tokyo, and, alas, discontinued in 1988.

*W*ith the exception of interchangeable lenses and trendy automatic focusing, there isn't much the hand-sized, seven-ounce XA doesn't offer. Its 35mm, six-element, D. Zuiko lens is sharp, fast, and forgiving, the XA variations offer operation from manual to fully automatic, and there's even a self-timer with a twelve-second delay for shy persons with an eye toward posterity.

*B*ut the best thing about the XA is the plump perfection of its shape, designed by Yoshihisa Maitani. Originally trained as an automotive designer, Maitani created the chassis of the XA using clay models, the classic approach to car styling. The result is a tiny camera that looks big, appealing to the hand as well as the eye. With its rounded shutter cover, the XA looks positively pregnant with possibilities.

No, no, they weren't the official foot-wear of an American squadron in the French Air Corps during World War I. Nothing half so romantic. They're just the plainest possible way for plain folk in the French countryside to protect their just plain feet. Espadrilles have been around in one form or another, cotton body and rope sole, for at least a couple of centuries. It's just crazy luck that they happen to be so compatible with the flawless teak on the decks of yachts, and that they make you look like the heir to the throne of Albania. *T*his recent model adulterates the classic style with the addition of a little rubber on the soles, just in case you find yourself on a surface rougher than teak, but there's nothing wrong with having one pair last the whole summer, is there? Two essential elements in espadrille drill: no socks, please; and be good enough to get at least a slight tan before going public with your ankles.

*T*o the *uninitiated, golf is just an-*other game, and not a particularly sensible one at that. But for lots of men in bright plaid Bermudas and women with skin like Florentine leather, the beauty of golf is not so much in seeing the ball roll at last into a devilishly small hole, but in exerting control over the sublime physics of the parabolic arc. How phenomenal that with a minimum of contact between ball and club, even a man in silly pants can tune in on the sublime music of the spheres.

*T*he ball, of course, is the key to this harmonious conjunction, and it is no mean piece of technological harmony itself. With its dense elastic core and its seamless, shiny, near-impervious cover of white thermoplastic, it is like a perfect little planet. A new golf ball is as fresh and willing as a thing can be, somehow far more promising than a tennis ball, with its four-day growth of peach fuzz. What makes a golf ball such a designated hit, however, are its dimples. If you thought they were there to create a nonslip surface, add four strokes to your handicap. In fact, the dimples are what make golf balls take flight rather than scud along the ground the way they used to in the days when players wore plaid kilts and bashed smooth wooden spheres with carved tree limbs. When these early balls became scuffed and dented, the historical theory goes, they began to travel greater dis-

tances. Taking a cue from this natural tendency, along about 1898 some remarkably intuitive soul at the Spalding Company came up with the idea of evenly denting a ball all over, and the game literally took off.

*T*he secret is this: Each dimple on the surface of the ball acts as a tiny venturi chamber. As the ball moves forward, air passing over the concave surface of the dimple must speed up to cover the slightly increased distance, in effect creating a turbo boost. Since dimples also increase air friction, the latest in the Spalding evolution, the sensuously beautiful Top Flite XL, is the product of cleverly negotiated compromises between longer flight and greater drag (just like life). The aeronautical cabal of Chicopee, Massachusetts, purveyors of physics to the duffers and dazzlers alike, decided to add a few more dimples but to make them slightly shallower, thus eking out a few more precious yards in a desperately driven game where every inch counts.

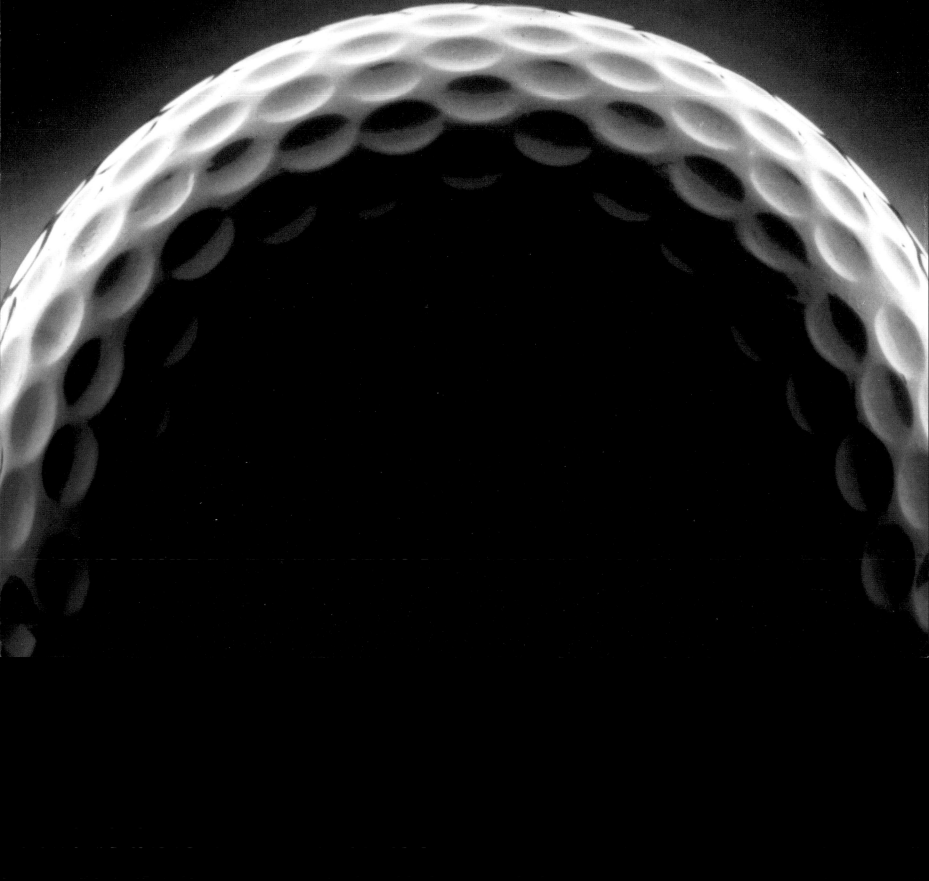

*Y*ou can *never be too thin, or know too* quickly how rich you are. What, then, could be more reassuring (and metaphorically right) than a calculator the precise shape and size of a credit card?

This is not the smallest calculator around—the nerd's delight is a tiny little wrist model with buttons that have to be pushed by dental instruments. But sheer gee-whiz miniaturization isn't the point. The surprise is that the film card is actually pleasant to use, in part no doubt because we have come to associate the shape and feel of the credit card with security and even respectability. Who could have imagined a few years ago that cash would come to seem untrustworthy and plastic would be the currency in which we would invest our emotions? Obviously, those lean and hungry minds at yon Casio, who brought microchip minimalism to working out your CD interest to seven decimal places by eliminating buttons and flattening the liquid crystal readout to a surface the color and thickness of a dime. With small size comes a cost, however: If you have more than $99,999,999 at any given time, you'll need something larger, like a heavyweight accountant.

*N*ot the least graceful of the film card's marvels is the photovoltaic cell that powers it, a tiny representative of a technology that deserves endless praise. Though a gaggle of geniuses contributed to the discovery and development of the photoelectric process, at the turn of the century a German physicist named Arthur Korn was the first to find a practical application of the phenomenon that certain compounds under certain conditions give off elec-

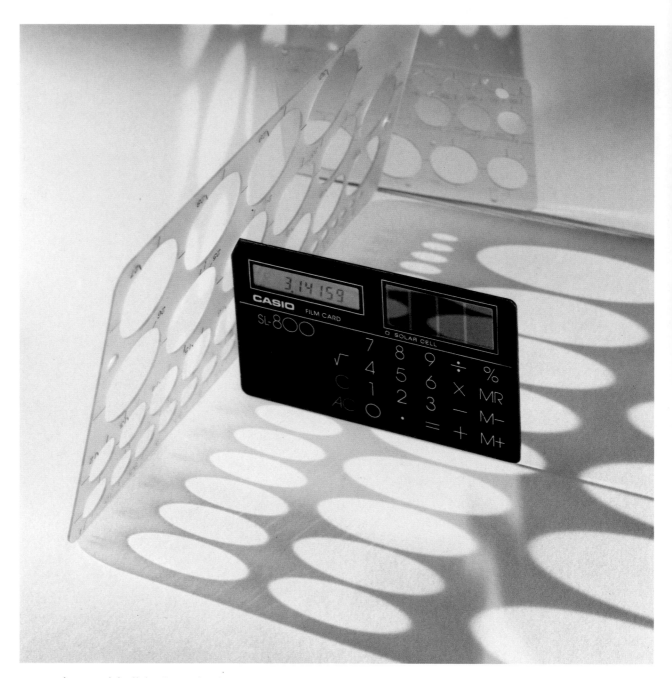

trons when struck by light. In 1954, scientists at Bell Labs managed to use Korn's idea to perfect the solar cell (a technology that may yet save us all). With no moving parts and a source of energy not likely to run out any time soon, the film card is about as close to the perpetual motion machine as we're going to get—*and* it can do square roots.

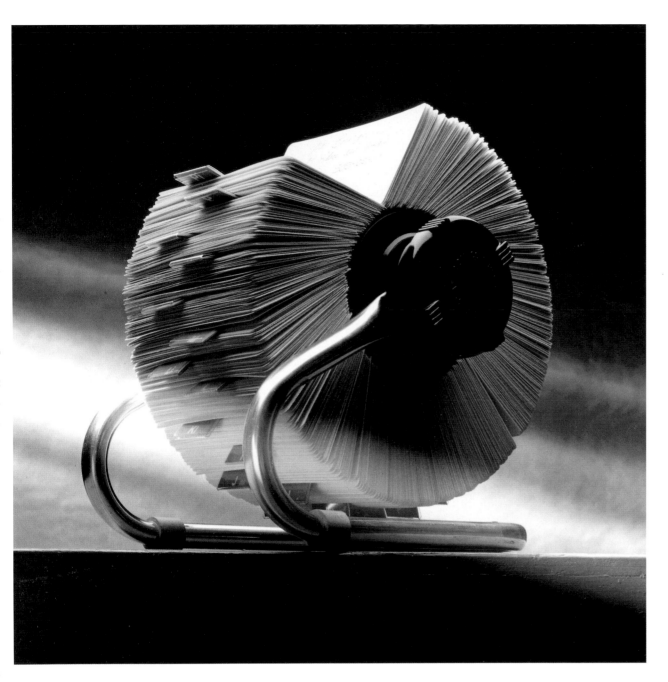

For corporate knights errant, there could be no better heraldic motto than "In Rolodex Is My Might." Invented in 1950 by Arnold Neustadter as an improvement on a primordial wheel of fortune called the Wheeldex, the device is nothing less than the singing sword of networking. Starting as a humble low-influence model with capacity for a few hundred cards (the "small circle of friends" training-wheel version), the thirty-two rotary files produced by the company reach a maxi-clout climax with the 6035X, a three-wheel intimidator that holds six thousand cards and costs more than two hundred dollars. Despite the fact that office computers can store more information and retrieve it with the tapping of a few keys, no desktop accessory so eloquently expresses the crucial business axiom, "It's not what you do, it's who you can call to do it for you."

*A*s if symbolic power weren't enough, Neustadter's masterpiece is a delight to use and behold, with its oversize handles, solid stance, gracefully curving aluminum tubing, and the meaningful ticking of its roller bearings. Most important of all, the Rolodex is a vivid daily reminder that, in business as in life, what goes around comes around.

What better symbol could there be of the anxiety and despair of the twentieth century than that little thumping heart of bureaucracy the rubber stamp? In Franz Kafka's chillingly imagined penal colony, a fiendish machine tattooed prisoners to death, but the complicated device was unnecessary since petty officials already had in their hands the means to stamp them out of existence. More recently, Saul Steinberg filled his ominous book, *The Inspector,* with the imprints of rubber stamps floating in the sky like dark moons. One way or another, the cosmic shadow of the rubber stamp hovers over us all.

*B*ut rubber stamps can be part of the solution as well as part of the problem. In the right hands they are handy indeed, able with a fine *kerthwok* to convey good news no less emphatically than bad. A rubber stamp can say, for instance, "Passed" and "Permission Granted" and (as here) the glorious "Paid." How sad that we so often see their work in such dreary phrases as "Payment Overdue," "Please Remit," and "Not Approved."

*T*his sine qua non of paperwork comes to us by way of China, where carved wooden printing plates existed as early as the T'ang Dynasty (A.D. 618–907) and artists have for hundreds of years signed their work with stamps called "chops." In the West, the devices used by nobles to put their marks in sealing wax evolved eventually into the minor official's ultimate power tool, helped along nicely in 1841 by Charles Goodyear's snappy process for vulcanizing rubber.

*F*or all its possible

misuses, the rubber stamp is an enormously pleasing technology to use, a microcosmic bit of the printer's art that has its own handcrafted magic. It's not hard to be good at rubber-stamping, any more than it is to *do* good with one. But each act takes some skill, and offers great satisfaction. After all, why shouldn't the rubber stamp be on the side of the angels as well as the bureaucrats?

We live in a time when human flight has been so thoroughly domesticated that flying machines are given names like Airbus, and seem so portly that one can hardly imagine how they get off the ground. Small wonder, then, that those of us inside ignore the Daedalean miracle of traveling at 600 mph and six miles aloft, instead munching little bags of peanuts, sipping diet sodas, and calculating our free mileage. Given such decadent behavior, it's fair to wonder if we deserve the ability to defy gravity at all.

*F*lying in the face of this dreary trend, thank goodness, is that great leap upward—the Concorde. A collaboration of British Aerospace Corporation and Sud Aviation that first flew in 1969, the 203-foot-long Concorde is small by the standard of, say, the 747 (which looks like an airplane designed by Botero) and only carries 144 well-heeled fast trackers. Environmentally, the plane makes no sense; though it can hit 1,350 mph, it gulps almost twice the fuel as its lumpen counterparts, makes a thunderous roar, and can't travel a mile farther than the *Spirit of St. Louis.* Who knows what it's doing to the ozone? And economically it's been pretty much of a bust, with only sixteen SSTs built before the project was terminated.

*B*ut with its gracefully swept wings and its dart-sharp nose, the Concorde—designed by Gordon Strang and Lucian Servanty—may well be the last romantic airplane, the final commercial vestige of a time when flight was fantastic, speediness was next to godliness, and "awesome" was not a word used lightly.

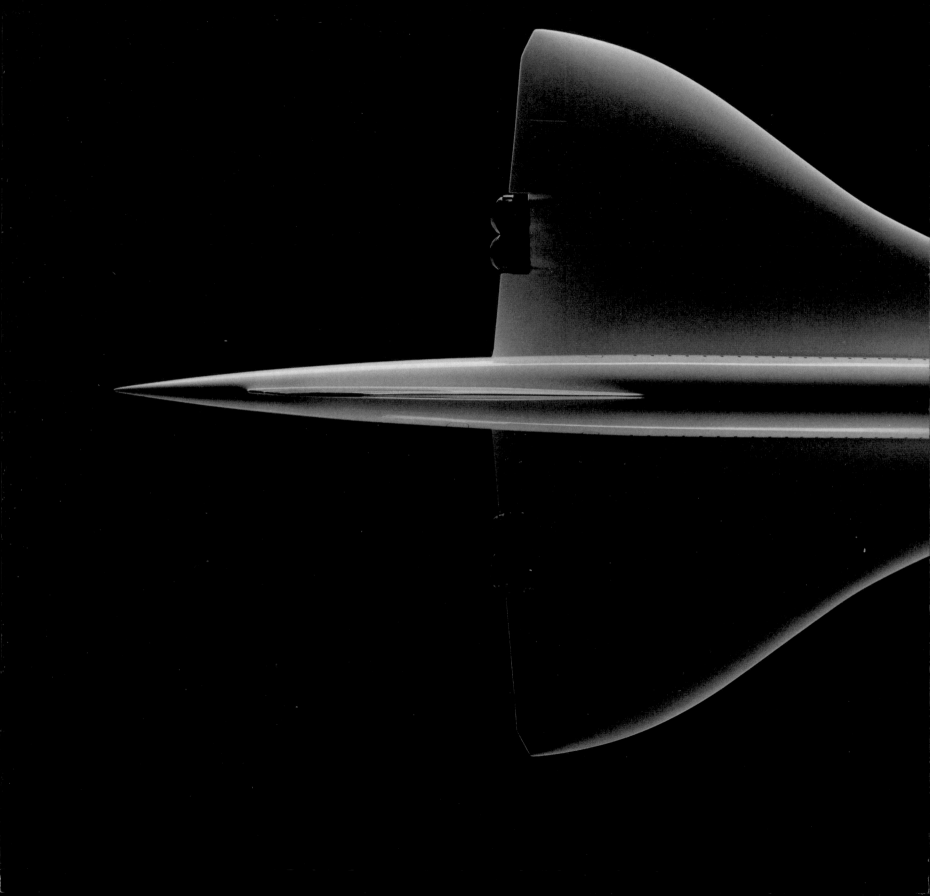

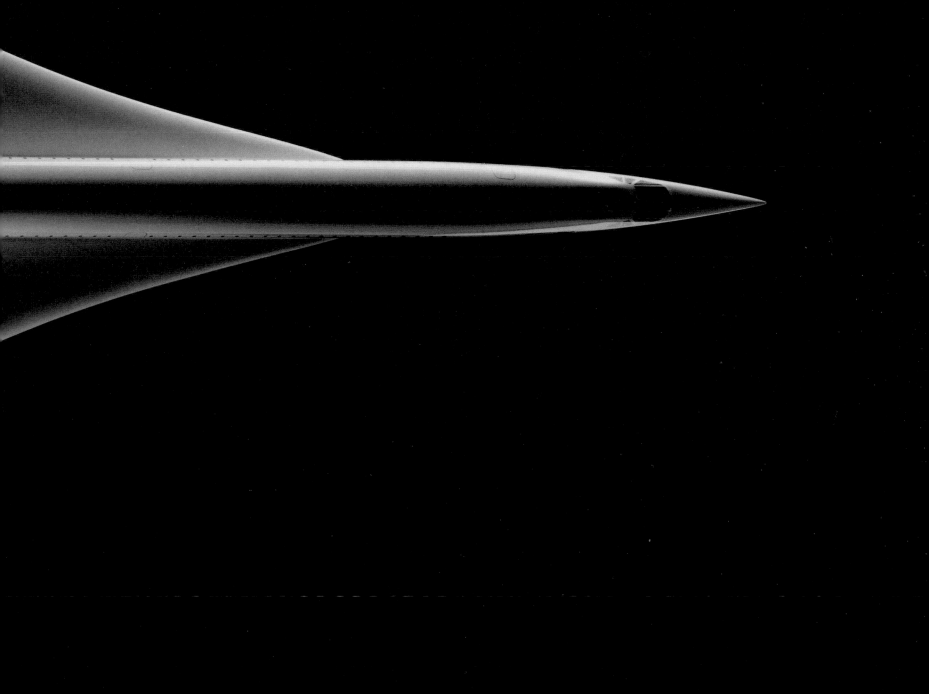

If a good measure of an object's value is the number of its uses beyond what it was meant for, the Dill's pipe cleaner, manufactured by United States Tobacco, in Greenwich, Connecticut, must be among the most estimable accomplishments of this century. Made for the express function of reaming out tar-clogged pipe stems—and made extraordinarily well for that thankless task—Dill's are nevertheless used for everything from minor construction to removing the accumulated dust of despair from authors' typewriters to the elaborate sculptural endeavors without which second grade would not be the hotbed of creativity it is.

*T*o say that the pipe cleaner passes little noticed through our pipes and through our lives is greatly to understate the matter. We assume that like rolled toilet paper or the brown paper bag, something as useful and dependable as the pipe cleaner exists because we have some natural right to have it; we accept as inevitable that our cars will break down from time to time, yet take for granted that pipe cleaners will never be less than perfect. To make amends, an appreciation is in order.

*J*ust how sturdy a Dill's pipe cleaner is can be demonstrated by trying to take one apart. You could unravel a Shetland sweater (or a Shetland pony) faster than you can defuzz a pipe cleaner. You can bend one back and forth twenty-eight times (more or less) before it breaks. The secret of this noble durability is a complex manufacturing process carried out by machines originally developed by the Ruf Machine Company, of New York City, that spin together two lengths of .018-inch steel wire and multiple strands of No. 6 pure, white, soft twist cotton (the machines actually produce two sets of double strands that are then divided by fixed-position knife blades). Trust me, you should know all this. A newly developed style incorporates tiny wire bristles using an even more complicated process, producing the crème de la ream, but as a sculptural material it's unfriendly. The machines (now located in South Korea) produce 58 feet of pipe cleaner, whereupon that mother lode is cut into 6¼-inch segments, and the whole thing starts up again, twisting the night away week after week and month after month in order to repopulate the world with estimable little Dill's.

For sensitive souls, chewing gum is a dispiritingly lumpen experience. After the teeth labor to soften a cardboardlike substance there comes a brief, flavorful interlude—as short-lived and sensational as cheap cologne—followed by countless repetitions of the same bovine jaw movement until the taste buds grow comatose and the thing in one's weary mouth grows old and ghastly gray.

*F*or years, the greatest minds in gum have tried almost anything to lure people past this "blah barrier" and make their product a cud above the rest. Bubble gum offers the incentive of lurid flavors like watermelon and banana, plus the chance to demonstrate at least one skill of great baseball players. A recent tactic borrowed from bonbons is to put a sweet liquid in the center of the gum, thus producing a burst of instant but ever-so-brief gratification. But these ploys appeal mostly to the young, and though one theory holds that some people can't walk and eschew gum at the same time, sophisticated adults tend to give the stuff up the minute they learn to pronounce cabernet sauvignon.

*O*nly Chiclets represent a successful evolution beyond gum's shortcomings, and only through Chiclets can grown-ups with a concern for style cling to the semiraunchy pleasures of gum. Introduced just after the turn of the century by the Warner-

Lambert Company, Chiclets possess an embarrassment of grace notes. First, a name derived from chicle, the coagulated sap of the sapodilla plant that is the key ingredient. Second, a gum-hither yellow-and-red package with a cellophane window out of which peek four of the dozen pieces, with the name emblazoned in *New York Times*-style type (all the chews that's fit to print). Most important of all—the crucial breakthrough—a thin, primer-white sugar coating that makes each piece as sleek as if it were designed in a wind tunnel and packs a satisfying al dente crunch that is as keen a thrill as gum can ever deliver.

Noguchi
L A M P S

The mere word lamp *can strike fear in* the heart. Born of the simple need to shed light on a limited area, this particular quest for fire has spawned the most extraordinary lumpen collection of peculiar objects since evolution came to the Galápagos. Bottles, driftwood, bulbous ceramic jars, stuffed birds, and a recent spate of variations on the coat hanger have all filled the need. But let's be honest—lamps are more endured than honored, more accepted as inevitable than loved. Almost without exception, they lack—if you will allow me—the light touch necessary to elicit affection. *T*he thorniness of the lamp problem may be the reason famous architects are constantly designing chairs but almost never take on what decorators call "area lighting." Let us all give thanks, then, that in 1951, the mayor of Gifu in Japan had the uncommon good sense to ask sculptor Isamu Noguchi to see what *he* could do about lamps in order to regenerate the town's moribund lantern business. What the ingenius genius could do, and did, was fashion wire, bamboo, and mulberry paper into a seemingly endless array of hanging or standing sculptures he called "Akari" (Japanese for "light" and "lightness"), creations so whimsical and imaginative that we can forget they're lamps and actually look forward to the long dark nights of winter.

While the boys in the Bauhaus were busying themselves making chairs that tested their theories of cantilevered construction or stress distribution, and incidentally providing the human body with some memorably uncomfortable places to sit, Alvar Aalto was off in Finland creating the sweetly curvilinear, anti-industrial Paimio chair.

*O*riginally designed in 1929 to be used at a tuberculosis sanatorium for which Aalto was the architect, the Paimio (also called the scroll chair) combines the spare structural integrity of an Adirondack chair with the high-speed élan of the streamline aesthetic. The chair is almost childishly plain, yet formidably sophisticated, with its armrests and legs fashioned of single pieces of bent birch (the indentation at the front clearly marking the change in function), and the scrolling at the top and bottom of the birch plywood seat doubling as decoration and cushioning springs. There is nothing arrogant or theoretical about the Paimio, just beauty and utility in a most delectable and imaginative form. Had she chanced to end up at Aalto's sanatorium, Camille would have looked awfully fine in one of these.

Aalto Paimio

S C R O L L C H A I R

*Nature abhors an unopenable con-*tainer. For instance, there could hardly have been a more difficult package than the giant armadillo, a Honda Civic–sized creature that passed this way during the Pleistocene age, but the formidable fangs of the saber-toothed tiger provided an opener not to be denied. In fact, the cat's exaggerated teeth were so specifically designed for shelling armadillos that when said species slouched toward extinction, the tiger's millennia were numbered. A similar symbiotic alliance of the closed and the opener spawned two simple but perfect tools to crack specific containers, and will soon turn them into fossils.

*T*he wire bottle opener, austere and perfect, was invented by William Painter of Baltimore and patented in 1894, around the same time he introduced the crimped bottle cap. The "can piercer" came along much later, in the early thirties, and is commonly called a church key—not because it is used with such religious zeal during televised Sunday NFL games, but because its early versions resembled, well, church keys. It was developed to offer the proper popper for the newly developed beer can, and, like the bottle opener, offers functional perfection with only one moving part—the user.

*Y*et for all their style and effectiveness, these worthy creatures are unlikely to see the twenty-first century. The technology that brought them into being has abandoned them: the screw-top bottle requires no opener, merely the grip of a professional wrestler; and the nail-breaking pop top has voided the need for the clean bite of the key. It is probably hopelessly retrograde

to point out that the screw top is a soulless bit of dull aluminum with none of the collectible crowning charm of a crimped cap, or that the pop top is configured so that you never get the last precious drops. Progress is cruel. And sometimes dead wrong.

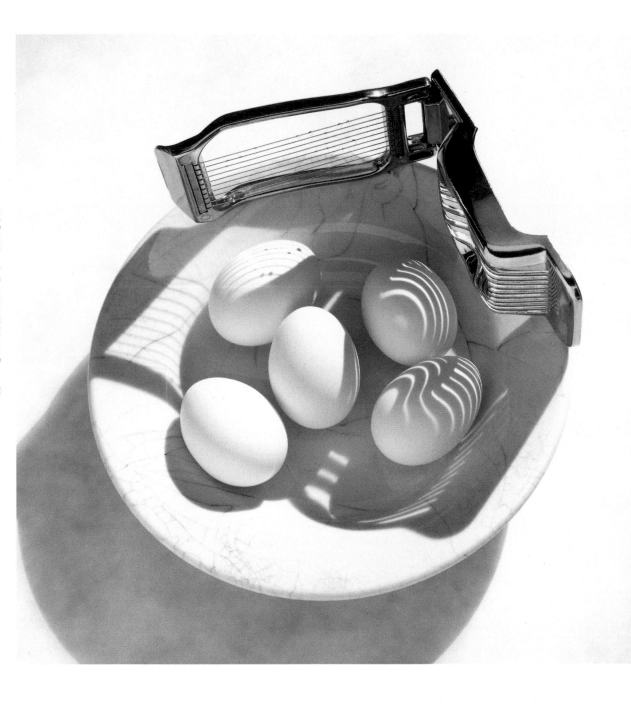

This elf's harp by way of Brancusi is elo- quent proof that the human mind will find a device for every task. Try to imagine a more perfect tool for a given purpose. To contemplate an egg slicer, with its wholly functional, entirely mysterious shape, is to stare straight into the bright heart of man's capacity to solve minor problems in poetic ways.

*T*hose who have sliced eggs by hand can testify that the job is nothing but pitfalls. The hard-boiled egg, with its odd combination of toughness, fragility, and differing textures, poses a consummate challenge to even the sharpest knife and the steadiest nerve. Using an egg slicer, however, like this beauty from Westmark in Germany, guarantees a near-perfect job every time. One smooth downward sweep of the taut wire blades produces yellow and white circles suitable for framing.

*T*he egg slicer has been around at least since the early thirties, when a cast-aluminum model was produced by Bloomfield Industries in Chicago. I have been around since the late thirties and can't remember a time when the little wonder wasn't working its magic in my life. My mother had a mystical belief in sliced eggs—they appeared in salads and sandwiches, atop our inevitable midweek macaroni casseroles, and regally adrift on wine-dark seas of black bean soup. How admirable it was to see her section egg after egg, with never a hint of malpractice. If only every slice of life since then had been half so perfect.

The eleventh commandment is well known: Thou shalt not put anything in thine ear smaller than thine elbow. Yet there is an undeniable compulsion to take something dangerously small and push it as perilously, deliriously, deliciously close to our tympanic membranes as possible. Call it madness, maybe the devil makes us do it, but we all stray from the path of righteousness, and we won't be stopped until the ear police kick in our doors and parade us down the street with funny signs around our necks.

*B*ut sin deserves to be done well (virtue being its own reward), and the unimpeachably right thing for this job is the Q-tip. For this infinitely useful, medicine-cabinet staple we can thank a man named Leo Gerstenzang, who in 1922 watched his wife wrap a tuft of cotton around a toothpick to clean their baby's ears and, in a flash of inspiration, realized that there were a lot of babies in the world, and they all had two ears. Armed with Gerstenzang's swab consciousness, Chesebrough-Pond's introduced the product in 1922 as Baby Gays (a name changed four years later to Q-tips Baby Gays, and finally—thank goodness—to its final form a few years after that). The *Q,* by the way, doesn't stand for quintessential, though it could, just plain old quality.

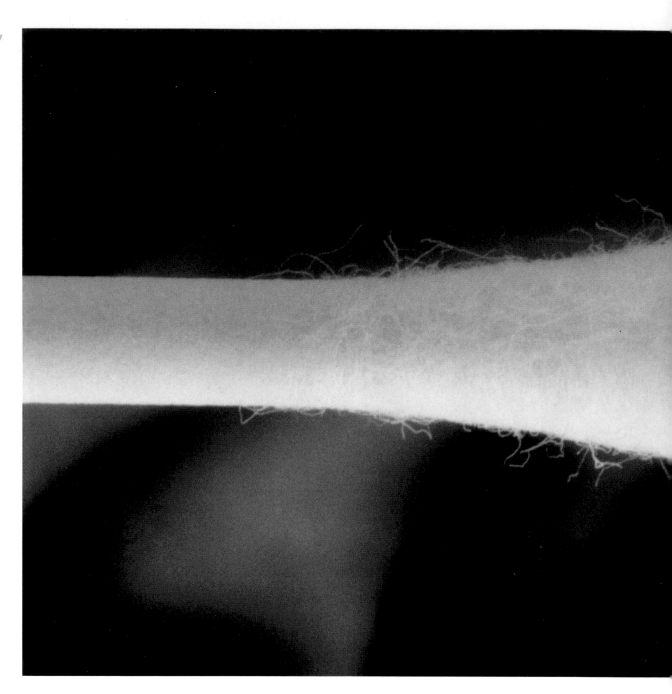

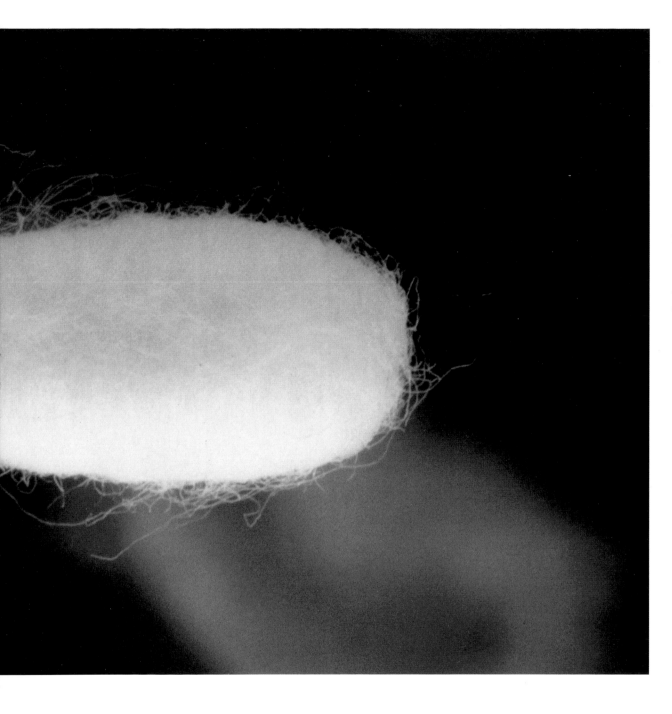

An immaculate replacement for all the pencils, matchsticks, bits of baling wire, et al., of the vast ear-cleaning underground, the Q-tip is nothing more than a 2⅞-inch wooden stick (or paper, for the cautious) with a beehive hairdo on each end. Nothing could be simpler, but try building one yourself, or using a substitute brand, so skimpily upholstered that the perilousness of the act becomes starkly evident. So go for the real thing; buy a few hundred thousand, just in case civilization takes a sharp downward turn. And never mind the disingenuous advice on the box that the "careful way to clean ears" is to "stroke [the] swab gently around the outer surfaces . . . without entering the ear canal." Even for an illicit act, there's such a thing as being *too* safe!

Uno-Vac

THERMOS

Don't stop me if you've heard this old joke: The distinguished experts at a famous think tank were trying to decide on the most extraordinary invention of all time. The obvious answers were offered: the wheel, the computer, the atom bomb, plastic, and so on. One member of the committee then suggested that they really ought to hear the opinion of the common man, so the elderly janitor was brought into the room and asked what he thought. The answer was immediate: "My Thermos jug."

*A*nd what makes the Thermos so special? the committee wanted to know. "In the winter," the man replied, "it keeps my cocoa hot. And in the summer, it keeps my lemonade cold." But why does that make it the greatest invention? the thinkers demanded. The janitor looked at them wonderingly. "How do it know?"

*H*ow *do* it know? Sheer brilliance. The mirror-bright reflecting surface painted on the inside layer of the double-glass container simply reflects back much of the heat or cold. Radiation is further diminished by a vacuum between the bottle's two leaf-thin layers of glass. Never mind that nature abhors a vacuum, it's done wonders for those of us whose idea of roughing it is a picnic in the park.

*W*e can credit an Italian inventor named Torricelli for the vacuum theory, which he posited in 1643. But we really owe our hot cocoa and cold lemonade to Sir James Dewar, who in 1892 invented the first vacuum flask for maintaining the temperature of laboratory liquids. (The invention wasn't an immediate hit: When Dewar brought one home to keep his infant son's milk warm, the inventor's mother-in-law was so doubtful she knitted a form-fitting wool cozy.) A German manufacturer produced the first "Dewar flasks" for home use in 1904, and ran a contest to find a new name for the device. Thermos, the ancient Greek word for heat, was the winner. And after eight decades, the dutiful and knowing Thermos is still a winner, making a moveable feast of the warm magic and cold comfort alike. The Uno-Vac, a steel cylinder with a handy handle that appears capable of surviving a fall from spectacular heights, has given the delicate technology of the Thermos its most potent incarnation.

Alcoa

The austere cylindrical perfection of the ubiquitous aluminum can ranks high on the all-time honor roll of best packages, along with the clamshell and the bikini. A six-pack of Dom Perignon to Alcoa, whose state-of-the-art can represents both an historic achievement in metallurgy and an ever-fresh approach to the preservation of food and drink. Aluminum itself, though the third most common element in the earth's crust, doesn't actually occur in nature as a metal, but only as parts of other compounds (sapphires and rubies, to name two impressive examples). The original extracting process, developed early in the nineteenth century by Danish chemist Hans Christian Oersted, was so expensive that aluminum was originally considered a semi-precious metal. Not until 1896 was a cheap method discovered, after which aluminum began showing up everywhere. (Even tinsel is aluminum these days, but for obvious reasons no one calls the stuff aluminumsel.) Its use as a container for beer and soft drinks has created a near-unimprovable design (except for the ill-conceived pop top), though some architectural changes in the last few years seem to reflect a postmodernist need to tart up its pure lines. This recent model's ziggurat top might seem a bit too droll for devout canimists, but it's a thoroughly modern receptacle for such avant garde potions as Gatorade, a wetter-than-water concoction named after a football team named after a classically designed reptile.

Perhaps
we should stop fretting about
our figures and admit the truth: we all
want ice cream, we want it now, and we
want it in nice round scoops. One of the
great unheralded design challenges of
this century has been to come up with
the perfect utensil for mining balls of ice
cream without having to wait anxiously
until the mother lode softens up. This
challenge was met and mastered more
than forty years ago by the artful cast-
aluminum scoop created by Sherman
Kelly (with a little help, perhaps, from
an earlier Italian model). With a smooth
sweep, the scoop's precisely shaped bowl
picks up a graceful curl so sweetly that
even the greediest ice cream addict
senses an artisan's satisfaction.

*W*ith its sculptured
form, this essential utensil might be just
another kitchen decoration but for Kelly's scoop *de théâtre:* a central core of
liquid Freon to retain heat, so that a few
seconds under the hot water tap renders
the tool invincible against even the most
resistant glacier of mint chocolate-
chocolate chip ripple.

Zeroll

I C E   C R E A M   S C O O P

Brigg

U M B R E L L A

*E*ver stal-
wart, the great English brolly
is one of the most effective side arms ever
wielded by civilized man. To carry one
bespeaks forethought and practical intel-
ligence. Tightly furled, or in full pano-
ply against the elements, the umbrella
ably represents true Brit readiness for
anything and everything. There seem no
limits to the trust an Englishman will
put in this admirable device. In the book
A Bridge Too Far, Cornelius Ryan tells of
a certain Major Digby Tatham-Warter,
who, during the worst hours of the Battle
of Arnhem in September of 1944, carried his umbrella at all times. Walking
along under a fierce mortar barrage with
his brolly held over his head, the major
was warned by a fellow officer that an
umbrella wouldn't do him much good.
Tatham-Warter coolly replied, "Oh, my
goodness, Pat, what if it rains?"
　　*F*or all its pluck in
drizzle or downpour (if not mortar at-
tack) the umbrella seems to have origi-
nated in bone-dry ancient Egypt, but
not, as might be expected, as a protec-
tion from the sun. Instead, umbrella-
shaped forms probably were held over
the heads of kings to symbolize the sanc-
tifying dome of heaven, and then were
adopted by lesser nobles who wanted
their own piece of sky. Eventually, someone must have noticed how much cooler
life was under the ornamental domes,
and the umbrella as both a distinguish-
ing *and* practical device was born. By the

Golden Age of Greece, the umbrella (or parasol) had acquired its classic folding framework that allowed it to be opened and closed. Though such mildly embarrassing options as telescoping handles or automatic opening springs have appeared in the past several years, the fundamentally handsome black beauty from Swaine Adeney Brigg and Sons ("By appointment to HM Queen Elizabeth" and all that) has never been bettered, and need never be. With a Brigg in hand, warriors in the workplace can have a piece of Tatham-Warter's memorable éclat without ever having to hear mortars fired in anger.

*W*hen the
village smithies who build this
flawless blade in El Cajon, California,
claim that their knife is in a class by itself, it's no idle boast. Though its lines
and craftsmanship seem timeless, the
cutting-edge folding hunter was first introduced in 1963, tracing its pedigree to
the well-tempered blades produced at
the turn of the century by H. H. Buck.
By incorporating a locking mechanism in
the handle, the highly evolved modern
model deals cleverly with the infamous
tendency of folding knives to fold shut
unexpectedly and bite the hands that use
them. Like any good utility knife, the
Buck holds a keen edge and has a satisfying heft in the hand, but touches such as
Macassar ebony handles and bolsters
forged as a single piece of burnished
brass make this as handsome and generous a manufactured object as America
produces. The Buck folding hunter
model is better by far than it has to be,
but not flashy. It won't make you feel
bigger or bolder, just fit enough to
survive—in a style to which you're
accustomed.

Buck

F O L D I N G K N I F E

*S*hall we celebrate the indispensable Razor Point for its fallibility? Unlike most inexpensive modern writing tools, which for all their efficiency lack personality, the Razor Point exhibits the endearingly human trait of mutability. Use a basic ballpoint tipped by some armor-piercing material and it will produce the same line day after day until it dries up, never changing with age, making no accommodation to the user's style. But the ever-pleasing, always-personal Pilot—favorite of art directors too numerous and overpaid to mention—was designed to behave about as organically as a plastic product can. The pen's Japanese inventors, in their search for a tip that would resemble a traditional calligrapher's instrument, pondered the porous lotus root (Japanese inventors being inclined to do that sort of thing). To facilitate ink flow and keep the point thin, they imitated said root and developed a plastic tip penetrated by many near-microscopic holes. Combined with a specially concocted ink, the resulting pen is as fine a thing for a little over a dollar (at the moment, that is) as can be wished.

A brand new Razor Point is as sensuous to use as a classic ink pen, but can never blot, however wildly wielded. As the point ages, it lays down a variable-width line that ennobles the script of any scribbler. By the end of its career, the old and nobly worn Pilot leaves a romantically unkempt trail that would have been a feather in Byron's inkwell. And then it's time for the keen thrill of a brand-new one, and a new semester of creative handwriting.

Being a man used to be all perks: swinging from vines, making bloodcurdling noises, brandishing weapons, *and* being admired for it. Now the best a guy can hope for, all things going well, is the dubious privilege of paying for dinner.

And yet—as a painful reminder that men still belong to the same gender that produced Goliath, Achilles, Richard the Lionhearted, and Vlad the Impaler—every day, minute by minute, relentlessly, our beards go on growing, five o'clock shadows of our former glory.

Is this stubble greeted joyfully, as a proof of virility? Maybe by the swarthy swells on the covers of *Uomo.* But for men who shave regularly, the act of removing a day's growth is a persistent annoyance. Among other things, it causes us to face ourselves in the mirror at a god-awful early hour. Better to be scheduled for a duel at dawn than to scrape one's face while facing the music of time.

But thanks to a prince named King Gillette, and those who carry on his noble work, what once was torment is now altogether tolerable, almost—if not quite—a pleasure. This true hero of the working man was the son and brother of successful inventors who wanted to carry on in the family tradition but hadn't a clue what to invent.

While working at the Baltimore Seal Company in the 1890s, Gillette met William Painter, inventor of the cork-sealed bottle cap, who gave him the useful if none-too-original advice to invent something that would be bought over and over again. Gillette later recalled plowing through the alphabet looking for an idea. (A . . . abacus wax? B . . . baseball-bat brush? C . . .) Then one fateful morning in 1895, Gillette realized he was enduring yet another bad shave from a straight razor he could never manage to keep sharp. So it was C for cheek chic; he'd invent a pre-sharpened disposable blade, and have the world by the shortest hairs of all.

Six years passed before a successful process for producing blades was developed, using an ingenious machine invented by Gillette's curiously named partner, William Nickerson. The first safety razor, with 20 blades, cost five dollars, and a 12-pack of blades alone sold for a dollar. In the first year, 168 blades crossed the counter. The company grew steadily if unspectacularly until 1917, when the mobilized military ordered 3.5 million razors and 36 million blades. Gillette, man and manufactory, would never again just scrape by.

The leading edge Atra, with its pivoting head and utilitarian beauty, has evolved from red blades and blue, tried blades and true, to reach a state of near perfection. It's hard to imagine the Atra being improved upon, unless the never-dulling, everlasting blade—that Sasquatch of consumerism —really does exist.

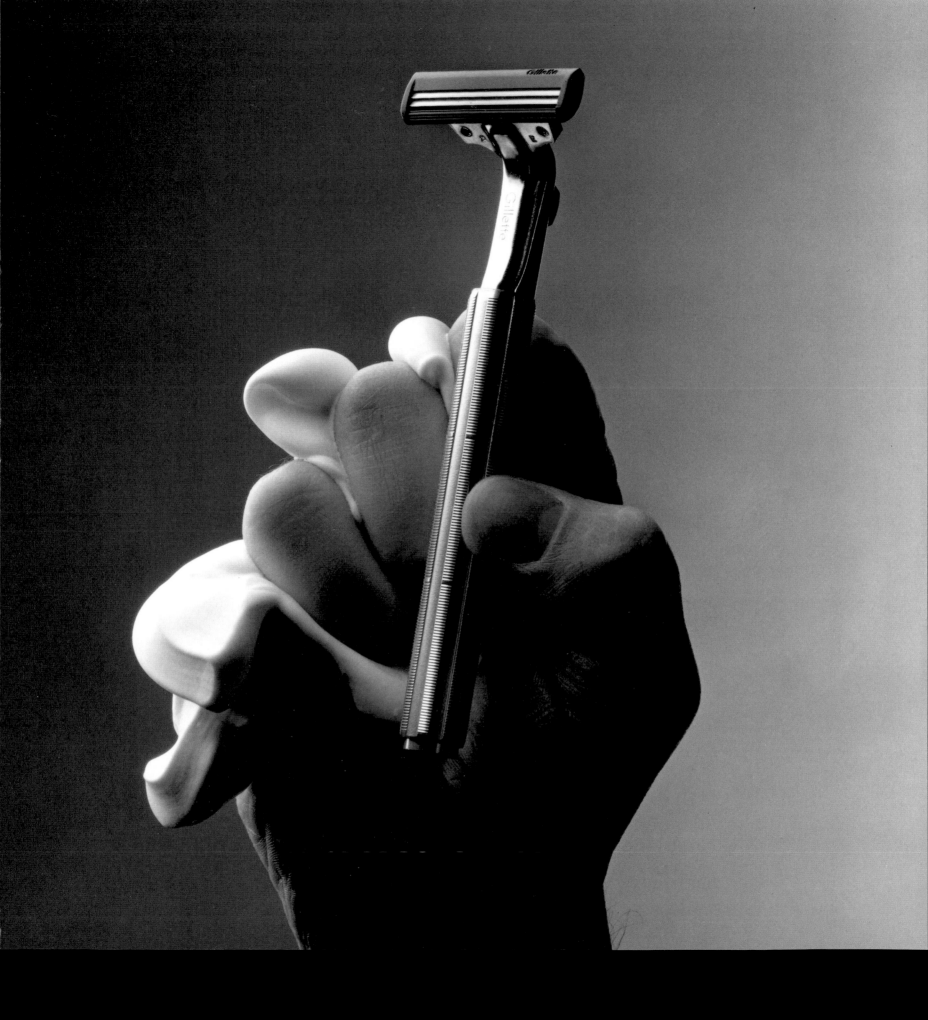

The venerable tux is striking proof that what's funky to one man may be high finery to countless others. Just a little over a century ago, tobacco heir Griswold Lorillard, weary of the tails required at evening functions, underwent a cropping operation to produce a comfortable version of formality for (almost) Everyman. Lorillard's friends were not amused at this descent toward cultural slough. But generations of men who look their dashing best in black tie owe this rebellious social lion everlasting thanks.

*T*he classic tuxedo must not, of course, be confused with the tuxedoid, any one of those ghastly hybrids of the seventies and early eighties that replaced the original's striking chiaroscuro with Necco-wafer shades of pink, blue, lavender, and other unholy hues. Weddings began to look like conventions of sorbet salesmen, and the point of the tuxedo—to lend a muted background of masculine austerity to the dazzling spectrum of women's dresses—was lost. But black is back, in response to a yearning for the psychic comforts of good form. The tuxedo, in its pure, dour splendor, has resumed its rightful place at the height of fashion.

*S*o three cheers for Lorillard's common touch, which has given us all the chance to dream in black and white. And a moment of thanksgiving that he was from Tuxedo Park, New York, and not Grosse Pointe, Michigan.

 To admire barbed wire is not easy. Its reputation has not been burnished by the misuses of the twentieth century. And remember what it did to your favorite Levi's? There's an aggressive nastiness about what cattle-country cognoscenti call "bobwire" that can make it seem personally malevolent. But let's look at the positive side: Before barbed wire made it possible for ranchers to selectively breed their herds, any bull could put the moo on any cow, and the devil take the rump roast. For all the range wars that erupted because suddenly there was another side of the fence for the grass to look greener on, at least barbed wire brought some discrimination to the love lives of cattle, and the future boast of "Billions and Billions Served" was unknowingly assured.

*T*hank Joseph Glidden for both the bad and the good. Though the idea of barbed wire had been around for a while, Glidden was the first inventor to apply for a patent, in 1873, for a two-strand design immodestly called Winner. Since then, hundreds of other wire styles have appeared, including the particularly vicious anti-personnel version called razor wire currently seen on better battlefields. The dazzling array of patterns has made barbed wire a hot collectible for those weary of competing for the lesser works of Cranach the Elder. Sotheby's has yet to hold an auction of important wire, but surely the Franklin Mint is keeping an eye on dependable old Bob.

B A R B E D   W I R E

*I*n one of *his radio reminiscences, Garri*-son Keillor recalled that for some years after his childhood he thought Vicks Va-poRub was a Lutheran product because of his mother's reverent air when apply-ing it to his feverish chest. Verily, Vicks *is* one of those products with a mysterious healing quality not fully explained by its ancient herbalist's ingredients (camphor, menthol, eucalyptus oil, cedar leaf oil, myristica oil, and other such earthy de-lights). There's something holy about this redolent gray glop, despite the fact that it has been produced for most of this century by staunchly secular Richardson-Vicks, of worldly Wilton, Connecticut. One can almost imagine a close reading of the gospels revealing that the three wise men arrived at the manger bearing gold, frankincense, myrrh, and Vicks.
*T*he particular wise man responsible for Vicks was a North Carolina pharmacist named Lunfford Richardson, who decided in the 1890s that the best treatment for his kids' croup was the above-mentioned potion. After treating his own children with it for years, he sold his pharmacy and went into business selling Vicks Croup & Pneumonia Salve (named after his brother-in-law Vic—obviously "Lunff's" wouldn't do—or after a seed company called Vicks, take your pick). The term *Vap-O-Rub* came along in 1912 and was streamlined at a later date, but nothing much else about the comforting stuff has changed since back when it was only the Richardson family's croup therapy.
*T*he chicken soup of WASP motherhood, Vicks is a deep-reaching restorative that relieves more

than the distress of colds. When things get especially dicey, one sure quick fix is to go to the medicine cabinet, pull out the numinous blue-and-green jar of Vicks, and take a long whiff—suddenly you're tucked up in a crisp white bed, with Mom reading you *Goodnight, Moon.* So let Zen macrobiotic snobs have their Tiger Balm. Vicks is the true-blue ointment of distinction.

*M*ost au-
tomobiles these days are efficient, dutiful, and drab. Though a few
cars retain the capacity to arouse, their
sex appeal often seems added as an after-
thought, like a librarian's eye shadow.
The Porsche 911SC is a creature apart, a
wheeled beauty that you want to throw
yourself upon, sobbing, biting, licking,
and agreeing to anything as long
as it agrees to be yours.
*T*he 911 is the last
of the chariots of fire that swept hero-
ically across the sixties. The Jaguar XKE
is long gone, the Aston Martin is rara
avis (exceedingly rare at Avis), the Ferrari
post-Enzo has changed everything but its
red paint, and the once-singular Cor-
vette now looks much like all the other
leading wedges. But the 911, first introduced in 1964, though faster and better,
remains instantly recognizable as the de-
scendant of the classic spoon-shaped
Porsche 356. No other car in the world
looks anything like it except, ironically,
its stubby half brother, the Volkswagen
beetle. Both designs have the same fa-
ther, Dr. Ferdinand Porsche, who started
out fashioning engines for Mercedes, created the preternaturally persistent "people's car" in 1934, and after the Second
World War dreamed up the car that
dreams are made of.
*F*rom the begin-
ning, the Porsche had a kind of no-

artificial-ingredients streamlining that
made it lovable as well as laudable, and
the 911, designed a quarter century ago
by the good doctor, hasn't lost that original charm while gaining formidably in
power and handling. Never mind that by
the time most people can afford one
their reflexes are not what they once
were; it's still nice to know that long after you've stopped performing at your
peak, your 911 will still be right up there
with Pegasus. So whether or not it matters, in our safe-and-sane age, that a tur-
bocharged Porsche can break 170 mph or
hit 80 in under ten seconds, just knowing you're driving a machine capable
of such stats is the standard equipment
of romance.

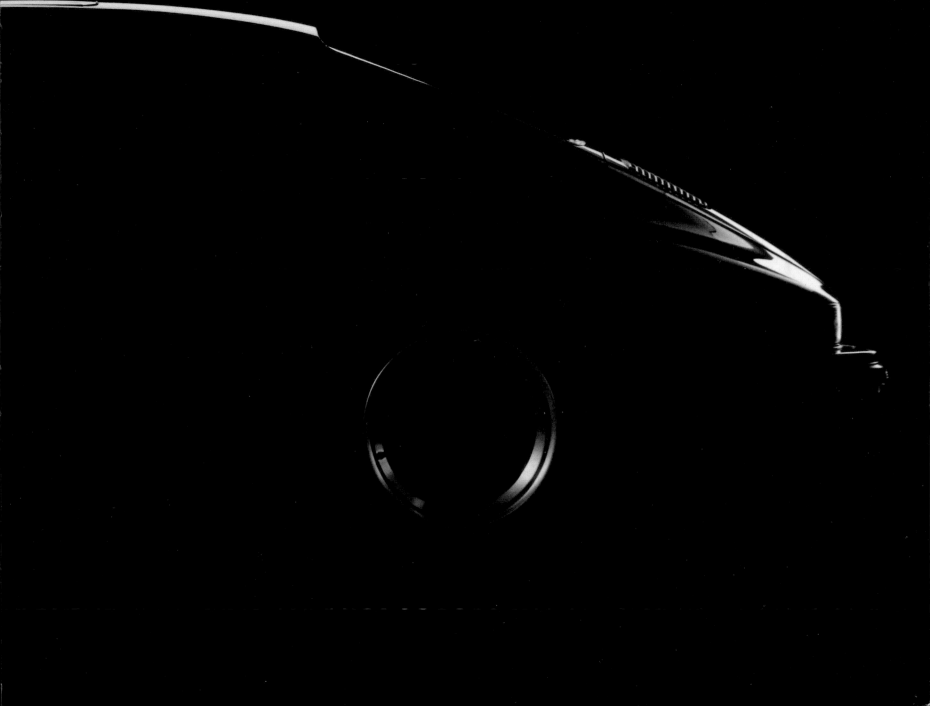

Black Flag
ROACH MOTEL

In a beauty and talent contest among earth's species judged by neutral observers from some other place altogether, there's no reason to assume *Homo sapiens* would come out ahead of the ancient and admirable family *Blattaria,* generally known as roaches. Given the many attributes of the roach, in fact—speed, agility, energy, efficiency, adaptability, and a hyperactive love life—it's quite surprising that evolution didn't stop right there. *W*hich prompts the question: Could simple jealousy be the reason we so relentlessly wage war on roaches? Or is it just plain territoriality? Give a roach an inch—or miss one by an inch—and it will show up next day with a bunch of friends and their hungry families. Annoying behavior, if not much different from the way humanity has overrun the planet. Whether or not roaches deserve our hatred, it's not morally wrong to wish they'd stay in the Amazon Basin and out of *our* basins. The trouble is, everything we think of to fight them—other than the unbeatable but messy swat—they learn to live with. After a generation or two they can eat the worst poisons we can concoct and suffer no more than a little heartburn. By trying to destroy them we end up building better and better roaches.

beach

*H*appily (for us, that is), the strategic thinkers at Black Flag had a better idea: the Roach Motel. It's a concept worthy of Alfred Hitchcock: Lure them in with promises of three-star cuisine, then stick them to the floor so they don't go home to make more roaches. As the Batesian ad copy (that's Norman Bates, not Ted) reads, "Roaches check in, but they *don't* check out!" By the time the No Vacancy sign lights up, you'll be able to revel in the satisfaction of a successful host. And the beauty of it is that no poison is used, so unless roaches develop Teflon feet, we can do them in without doing them any genetic favors. Of course the decor, with that tacky fake-wood grain, makes the place a bit sleazier than you might wish, but as long as customers keep dropping by, why redecorate?

Radius D.D.S.

MOUTHBRUSH

*P*resumably the idea of scraping odd bits and pieces off one's fangs dates back to a time when men were men, meat was tough, and Novocain was a hard rock briskly applied to the side of the head. Records of implements designed specifically for cleaning teeth begin in China and go back at least as far as 1600. By 1728, a French dental surgeon named Pierre Fauchard was decrying prototypical toothbrushes as expensive novelties "in the nature of textile mops," and recommending instead the use of certain herb roots and wet sponges. (The Fauchard effect may be why the French still have the most neglected *dents* in Europe.) The toothbrush that launched the Age of Intimacy—a length of bone to which boar bristles were secured by wire—was designed in 1780 by an English saint named William Addis. In essence, the thing hasn't changed all that much since then, except for the development of angled heads, synthetic bristles, and lurid colors. Then, proving the idea that if you build a better mouthtrick the world will eat a path to your door, along came the Radius D.D.S.

*T*his breakthrough brush got its start, apparently, when James Havard, an abstract painter with a photo-realist appreciation of fermented beverages, awoke one morning in a state of disrepair and longed for a brush of industrial strength. He mentioned the problem to a friend, designer James O'Halloran, who began to envision a toothbrush with heroic proportions and hygienist-in-a-drum power.

*S*omehow, the resulting Radius makes desirable putting into your mouth a brush that might

seem more appropriate scrubbing your car's upholstery. A large handle designed with a thumb rest provides the kind of leverage one associates with a deep sea fishing rig, and 3,588 nylon bristles (count 'em) cut a wide swath through the oral blahs. The D.D.S. looks meaningful, for one of the most meaningful jobs in civilized society.

From Adam to Yves, couturiers both haute and not-so-haute have worked to overcome both nakedness and serious overdressing, trying to find the perfect blend of simplicity, utility, and taste. It seems almost cruel to tell those still engaged in the struggle that the ultimate in purity has been there all along. Or at least since the Bronze Age, when people really knew how to dress. Clothing on a mummy found in a Danish peat bog dates back that far, and one piece has the unmistakable tubular body and short sleeves of the classic tee (lacking only the words "Kiss Me, I'm Nearly Civilized" to make it thoroughly modern).

*T*he T-shirt has an endearing incipience about it; it looks like a person just about to happen. As basic as clothing can get—right up there with the sock and the mitten—the to-a-tee tee is nothing less than elemental.

*O*f course, there are tees and there are tees. Anything other than 100 percent cotton is simply wrong, and such things as sayings, corporate logos, or pictures of Madonna and Samuel Beckett (whether together or separately) are a distraction from the impeccable line. Too tight is too tacky, and though loose as a burnoose is just now the epitome of style, about one size too large is really the best. Of all the countless thousands of T-shirt types, the purest of all is the good gray gym shirt, like the old champion from Champion, which lasts forever, ends up as soft as chamois, and garbs you in Spartan glory.

Champion

T - S H I R T

*The basic sliverware of the East repre-*sents an entirely scrutable design idea, and a subtly influential one. The dexterity required to use chopsticks adds grace to an act that elsewhere threatens to descend into savagery at the drop of a fork. Once you have mastered chopsticks, eating Oriental cuisine with anything else is like playing polo on a Clydesdale.

*E*quipped with a fork and a sharp knife, an ambitious diner can launch confidently into an entire large roasted creature, as some of our forebears were inclined to do. But with the limited carrying ability of chopsticks, decorum is virtually guaranteed. Though an Oriental officeworker on lunch break can move his sticks at a blur (*chop* being pidgin English for fast), the general tendency is to eat in measured mouthfuls. And while the presumptuous gourmands of the West might assume that a pair of sticks are somewhat primitive, back when proto-Parisians were still at the tooth-and-nail stage of etiquette, a Chinese diner would have shuddered at the idea of touching his food with anything less *raffiné* than a nicely tapered set of chopsticks.

*T*he **ground-to-a-powder pepper** that comes in a can at the supermarket is poor stuff, more like a chemical imitation than the meaningful East Indian condiment *Piper nigrum* itself. To retain its fine, unrefined ferocity, pepper has to be ground on site by a machine suited to the purpose. The grandest grinder of all is not one of those elephantine chess pawns with which overbearing waiters bring dinner conversation grinding to a halt, but the little pewter Perfex made in Saint-Etienne, France. This squat device has a pleasantly machine-age look, fits comfortably in the hand, grinds relentlessly with the turn of its nicely leveraged handle, and refills through an ample trap door (allowing the chore to be done by little kids who need some key responsibilities but can't yet be trusted to dry the blown-glass champagne flutes).

*S*o many manufacturers produce this wonder, including Muhle in Germany and Peugeot, also in France, that it's hard to know which country to credit. But whether it first did its dependable work on *poivre* or *Pfeffer*, the marvelous mill has been a hot property with *schönen Müllerinnen* ever since.

Perfex Bijou

P E P P E R   M I L L

General Electric
L I G H T   B U L B

Everybody knows, of course, that Thomas Alva Edison invented the light bulb. Which is nice, except that he didn't. If one wants to be an absolute stickler for chronological fact, and naturally one does, an Englishman named Joseph Wilson Swan was the first to produce a working electric light bulb. Swan theorized in 1848 that a constant electric current in a vacuum might create light. Thirty long, dark years later he demonstrated a working model, almost a year before Edison saw the light. But marketing is everything. Edison's theatrical coup of lighting the streets of Menlo Park, New Jersey, his hometown, put the English competition in the shade. Which is why New Yorkers today pay their light bills to Con Edison, not Con Swan.

*D*espite occasional reminders of the miracle of electric light—usually when the bulb burns out in the bathroom—almost nobody praises the sheer beauty of the light bulb itself. Not much has changed in its appearance since Edison's and Swan's elemental bright ideas. Edison's prototype burned for forty hours, while today, with some luck, you can get twelve hundred hours out of one. But except for the sleek mirror reflector, the GE bulb pictured here bears a remarkable resemblance to its ancestors of a century ago, its pressure-resistant gourd shape reminiscent of ancient blown-glass bottles. Through the clear section, you can glimpse the heart of the matter: a wisp of filament, glowing with the desperate desire to burn up but deprived of the hint of oxygen that would make self-immolation possible. We may not completely understand it, but seeing is still believing.

National flags are to art what national anthems are to music. They are meant to swell the spirit with the vision of patriotism, "My country 'tis of thee" and such. Simply put, what flags stand for is "Our Side Uber Alles." Or, as Mel Brooks's two-thousand-year-old man proudly sang, "Let 'em all go to hell, except Cave Seven." Given this ungenerous sentiment, it's not too surprising that most flags are aesthetic calamities. The best that can be said for many is that they attempt very little, merely placing one rectangle of color next to another and usually stopping at three. Some go in for a kind of symbolic realism that usually falls flat. The flag of Wales displays a rather unlikely dragon, while Lebanon's cedar tree seems right out of a Disney background. The USSR's hammer and sickle is a drab drape proclaiming all work and no play (if you're lucky). And as for the Stars and Stripes, it seems that Betsy Ross, Our Lady of the Busy Pattern, couldn't decide *what* to do, so she did a little of everything.

*T*he truth is that all flags, having provided cover for centuries of unspeakable behavior, should probably be viewed askance. But as a near-perfect work of design, the flag of Japan deserves a smart salute. For centuries Japan, with its countless warlords and endless factional disputes, was as flag-happy as a Republican National Convention. But after Admiral Peary's famous getting-to-know-you visit, the Japanese decided they needed a single flag to identify their merchant fleet. The Betsy Ross of Japan was Lord Nariakira Shimazu, head of the powerful Satsuma clan of southern Japan, who prevailed upon the government to adopt the ancient motif of his clan's banner. Since the country's proper name, Nippon, means "source of the sun," Shimazu's choice clearly made sense. With its graceful geometric simplicity, the flag is a prime example of Japanese understatement in design. (Its proportions have been exactly stipulated since 1870: A white rectangle measuring ten units by seven, with a red circle measuring three-fifths the rectangle's width, placed one one-hundredth of the rectangle's length closer to the pole edge than the outer edge.) When an art director who was designing posters for the Tokyo Olympics suggested making the sun larger, the response was an indignant turndown. The Japanese may have a hard time pronouncing "Leave well enough alone," but they know when they've got something that doesn't need any fixing.

*F*or Americans to appreciate this flag as a design when we have so many conflicting associations with what it stands for is not a particularly easy task. Perhaps if we thought of it as a Jasper Johns . . .

Matchbox

*O*nce *upon a time, when God was in* His heaven and Ozzie and Harriet were in theirs, a new car every year or two was a proclamation that all was right with the family. The autumnal introduction of the new models from Detroit brought passionate debate within families over whether tradition would be maintained if, say, a new Buick sporting useless oblong holes above the fender replaced last year's model with the useless round holes. Or over whether this was the year to give Oldsmobile a try, or even make the great symbolic leap to Cadillac. For Dad, Mom, Chucky Junior, and Betty Sue, car buying was an almost constant preoccupation, and the mysterious smell and take-me-I'm-yours excitement of the new car were always with us.

*S*uch halcyon reassurance is gone now, or at least far rarer than anyone could ever have imagined in the chrome-sweet-chrome days of the fifties. Buying a new car has become a dour exercise in consumer research that comes maybe two or three times a decade. Cost efficiency and coefficient of drag have replaced ego gratification, and another of life's fine frivolous pleasures is no more.

*Y*et for a couple of dollars (and no monthly payments) anyone hungering for the thrill of virgin wheels on a regular basis can bring home a shiny new Matchbox car. All you need for an excuse is a kid (a niece or nephew will do) and you can indulge your lust, thanks to the tiny little designers and engineers in Moonachie, New Jersey. One might think that all toy cars are pretty much alike, but one would clearly not have driven a Matchbox Aston Martin or '56 Chevy hemi across the dicey surface of the dining room table. With leaf-spring suspensions, immaculate hand finishing, rubber tires, and a connoisseur's choice of the latest (and greatest) models, Matchbox makes the best Lilliput-putts of all—which is why seventy-seven million of them rolled off the company's assembly line last year. Iacocca, eat your heart out.

Softball is not a hardball gone to flab. It is a stately creature, on the plump side, with all the presence of good Sir John Falstaff or a derriere by Rubens. Or at least that's what it ought to be. In fact, most softballs just don't get the look, the special aesthetic; they end up as distended baseballs, and when you catch one you feel like a little kid whose hand is too small. But the nonpareil Clincher F12, invented in 1934 by Frederick deBeer, has the archetypal softball look. And feel. In fact, the Clincher truly defines the softball and might just as well be the only one produced. Made with a cork core wrapped in heavy cotton string impregnated with rubber and covered with white leather, the Clincher is plenty hard, the way softballs ought to be, and quite large, but not dauntingly massive. What singles it out as a technological achievement is its stout resistance to having even the neighborhood bully knock the cover right off it. The clever Clincher has extra-long stitches and a special design that hides the usual Frankensteinian seams and gives the ball its unmistakable organic appearance. There is an endearing dignity about the Clincher that makes it the kind of ball you simply want to be seen with.

Kaypro

*A*t the
moment this note of praise
and gratitude for a computer is being
written on my trusty keyboard, the Kaypro II is so far from state-of-the-art that
it's nearing a state of antiquity. When it
was first introduced in the early eighties,
the Kaypro could remember sixty-four
thousand characters (almost as many as
populate "Dynasty") without writing
them down, which amounts to about ten
thousand not very fancy words. For writ-
ers, who often can't retain the punch
lines to three jokes, the feat seemed miraculous at the time, and the portable
Kaypro became the early favorite of people like William Buckley and Russell
Baker. Now computers are considered re-
tarded if they can't store ten times as
much as those old Kaypros—all the
punch lines for every joke ever cracked—
and recall it four times as fast.

*B*ut the venerable
Kaypro II, and its smarter successor, the
2X, produced by the Kaypro Company
in Solana Beach, California, has qualities
rare in the futuristic world of computers.

First, as a portable (though at thirty
pounds it should come with its own
Sherpa) it had the compact packaging of
a box turtle, with the keyboard doubling
as a lid. And in an industry that designs
most of its hardware to look like preten-
tious television sets, the gray steel Kaypro resembles a no-nonsense piece of
military gear, lending its words the
meaningful weight of ordnance. As dependable as it is unglamorous, the Kaypro hardly ever breaks down, ponders a
bit slowly but surely, and somehow en-
genders affection in a way the cool and
imperious IBM PCs never do. The VW

Beetle of computers, it's a homely classic
that by 2001 will surely have a special
niche in the final resting place of
cybernetic heroes, *Hal*halla.

*O*nly a *few thousand years ago, all* mechanisms were the sole property of nature, and knowledge of how they worked was best left to the gods. Then humans came up with their own machinery, and before we knew it we were privy to such hubristic wonders as the lawn mower, the steam engine, and the electric carving knife. Sometimes these machines got pretty complex, but you didn't need nerdthink to puzzle them out: the doohickey fitted into the gizmo, and so on. Sooner or later, just about any conglomeration of moving parts could be understood. But lately, machines are leaving us hopelessly behind. Electronic sorcery is changing everything, and in modern mechanisms hardly anything seems to move. When something goes wrong, call a witch doctor.

*T*hus the great comfort in something as resolutely mechanical as the El Casco pencil sharpener, manufactured by Eibar in Spain. With none of the grating noise and brute force of the modern office pencil processor, the handsome El Casco lets you view through a magnifying lens on top the workings of worm gears and blades as they manicure such treasures as Faber Mongol No. 2s and Dixon Flamingo No. 303s. With such amenities as a hefty handle, a pencil-gripping feeder, a removable shavings drawer, and a suction cup to hold things unshakably in place, noble Casco is a reminder that men and machines can still reach a workable understanding.

Daisy

B B   G U N

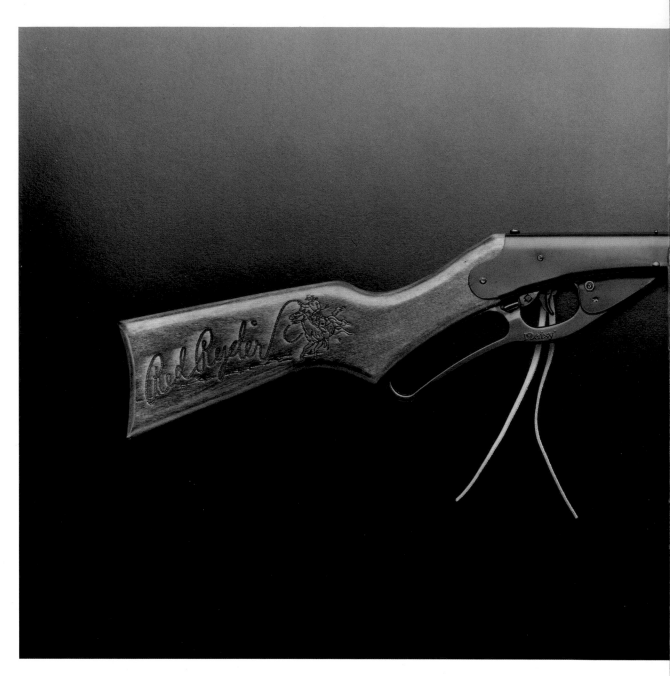

Once upon a time, in a fratricidal snit, my older brother cornered me in the cellar back by the coal bin, took aim with cold deliberation, and shot me in the knee. Years later, due to a miracle of twentieth-century technology, I walk without any trace of a limp. This wonder wasn't some phenomenon of medical science, but my brother's Daisy Red Ryder BB gun, a weapon serious enough to leave me stung, benign enough to let me off unmaimed. If only the fractious armies of the world were equipped with Daisys, and only Daisys, war could go on being as popular as ever without being so unpleasantly fatal.

*N*ot, of course, that the Daisy is intended for such aggressions. Among its various virtuous uses, in fact, is teaching kids *not* to shoot each other, by accident or otherwise. (Daisy's management naïvely hopes for a world free of desperadoes like my brother.) But since boys just want to have primal fun, the timeless act of hitting what you aim at has never lost its charm. And nothing makes a more satisfying plink on a man-eating can than a Daisy.

*B*ut why the unlikely floral name? Is this one of those newspeak euphemisms, like the nuclear missile dubbed "Peacemaker"? Not at all. The story goes that one day in 1888, Clarence J. Hamilton brought an air rifle he had designed to L. C. Hough, general manager of the struggling Plymouth Iron

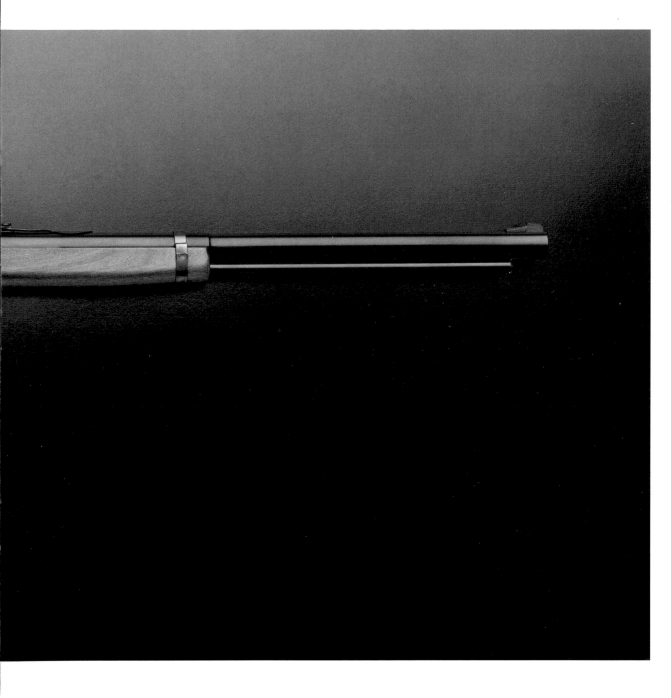

Windmill Company, in Plymouth, Michigan. Hoping that some sort of free gift might prove an incentive to local farmers to buy a windmill, Hough agreed to try the gun out. After putting a BB through a wooden shingle ten feet away, Hough fatefully declared: "Boy, that's a daisy!" The name stuck, despite macho competitors like Sterling, Prince, Atlas, and Matchless. The windmill business blew colder and colder, but farmers were more than willing to pay for air rifles, and ninety-eight years of steady sales have given Daisy a well-deserved pot shot at corporate immortality.

*I*n 1939, the company approached artist Fred Harman, creator of a comic-strip cowboy called Red Ryder, and bought the rights to use the heroic name on a new gun modeled on the classic Winchester lever-action 30-30. It was the best Daisy of all, and it's still around. For me, it was the gun that won the East, and when my brother Geoffrey the Kid finally rode off to college, Daisy was all mine.

*A**nyone who imagines that girls' camps** are places of genteel canoeing instruction, rainy-day lanyard making, and girlish voices singing "Because God mayade the ivy twine . . ." has never been to a girls' camp, except maybe to drop Amy off and head back to the pleasures of an empty nest. The author, however, has actually worked in a girls' camp, and has witnessed the volcanic sexuality ruthlessly suppressed, the moist palms, bad skin, and libidos twisted into strange shapes, the daydreams of Viking raids and girlish gasps at tales of unimaginable depravity. In such places, naturally, boys are kept at bay, and hunger tends to substitute for lust. Enter the legendary s'more, an infamous campfire confection made by putting a section of Hershey Bar on a graham cracker, topping it off with a marshmallow, and letting the whole thing melt over the fire until it is an obscenely wonderful sweet mess that leaves the little twisted sisters whining for "s'more."

*T*hat such a handcrafted sensation could be massproduced would seem too much to wish for, and yet behold the magical Mallomar. Created by Nabisco in 1913 by the cookie geniuses who had just developed the Oreo, the Mallomar changes the order of ingredients, with the chocolate on top acting as an edible wrapper for the rest, but it is a s'more, more or less, understandably venerated by a considerable cult following. The fact that the Mallomar has never been featured as a prize possession on "Lifestyles of the Rich and Famous" indicates clearly that high camp is woefully out of touch with girls' camp.

*I*tty-bitty *is the kind of adjective that* causes grown-ups to lose credibility with young children. It ought to be quarantined, locked securely inside icky books for toddlers and never allowed out. Any product that uses the term in its nomenclature might well be shunned without question. But despite its lamentable name, the "itty bitty" book light deserves nothing but praise. Why couldn't it have been called the Your Eyes Only light, or the Me, Myself, and I light? Oh, well, never mind, the "itty bitty" will just have to make it on its merits, which are considerable. Clipped to the back page of a book, the you-know-what light casts a pool of bright illumination just the size of a page, leaving everything else in darkness. In a flash, it revives the elemental bond between reader and page that was first forged when you sneaked a comic book under the covers after lights-out and read by the speleological glow of a flashlight.

*T*he Edison of this particular bright idea is Noel Zeller, owner of Zelco Products, who originally wanted to give himself a better light source for airline travel. And yes, Zeller must bear responsibility for the name, which he thought was catchy. But let's honor his innovation, not dwell on his limitations in the name game.

Zelco "itty bitty"

B O O K   L I G H T

Jeep
WRANGLER

In a strictly evolutionary sense, the dauntless Jeep isn't a car at all. Cars evolved from horse-drawn carriages and were called "horseless carriages." Since the Jeep (from GP, for general-purpose vehicle) was developed to replace the military motorcycle, which had replaced the courier's horse, the Jeep's direct line of descent is from four-legged, not four-wheeled ancestors. Thus it might be called "the horseless horse."

*T*hough the modern version is considerably larger than the World War II original, the Jeep retains the unfrivolous form of the motorcycle it replaced; it is pure transportation without an ounce of fat. But unlike such utilitarian shapes as, say, the hammer, the Jeep isn't the inevitable result of reductive design. After all, many countries have developed military runabouts, from the sardine-cannish little German VW reconnaissance car to the big desert-bashing English Land Rover, and none of them looks exactly like the Jeep. In fact, the first military vehicle developed by Willys Overland Company in 1940 for testing by the army, called the MA, didn't look much like the Jeep either, but rather like an undernourished military truck. In 1941, determined to extract the most from the least, Willys designers got it just right, and despite almost half a century of small changes, the inspired machine is still instantly recognizable as the ground-pounding GI it was born to be.

Ironically, the civilian Wrangler is the sole survivor of a long military line. The redoubtable war-horse has been led into the Chrysler stable, while the fickle Pentagon has turned to a new design improbably called the Hummer (a vehicle so lame, apparently, the troops have nicknamed it "the bummer"). But the jaunty Jeep, a road warrior whether or not there's a road, still delivers the kick that all the aero- and stereodynamic dream machines long ago took away. It's the last set of wheels that gives the word *horsepower* more than a statistical meaning.

Triumph

S A L A D S P I N N E R

Admittedly, the problem of drying lettuce doesn't compare to such weighty vexations as how to reduce the deficit or why it is you can't remember anything you saw on the seven o'clock news. But it *is* a bother. After all, lettuce must be washed, and has to be dried if salad dressing is to have its desired effect. Complicating matters is the fact that lettuce leaves aren't smooth, which would be convenient for salad makers, but is wrinkled and water-retentive in accordance with some mysterious plan that seems—perversely—to favor rabbits. Over the centuries this characteristic has inspired countless drying methods, from moderately successful to totally useless. There are those who insist on whirling a wire basket full of drenched lettuce in a circle, resulting in water-stained walls and extreme dizziness. A Greek woman who once had a meteoric career as a cook in my island house actually dabbed each leaf with a dish towel, which took a long time (as she no doubt intended) and imparted to her salads just a hint of cheap Athenian detergent.

Such drudgery might have led to the demise of salad altogether were it not for the ingenious use of centrifugal force employed by the Triumph salad spinner from France, the handsomest of several similar utensils that do the job with an admirably dry wit. The workings of this four-part invention employ some old Newtonian magic: an off-center handle turns a drive wheel in the top, which activates gears in the lid, thus transferring power to a basket in a . . . well, you get the idea. Hardly any effort is required to create a

Prospero-quality tempest in which water and leaf are separated absolutely, irrevocably, and forever. The impressive results are guaranteed. By law.

Estée Lauder

*S*culptor **Claes Oldenburg, who knows** what he likes, has erected a monument to the artful lipstick tube on the campus of Yale University, to which we may all say a grateful "Amen."

*F*rom this ingenious device arises the ritual gesture that so eloquently defines femininity: the careful double-arch tinting of the upper lip, the graceful sweep of the lower, the business-like blotting compression of the mouth, the winding back of the stick of Passionate Pink or O'Hara Scarlet, the satisfied replacement of the cap, and one last glance in the mirror for reassurance in a chaotic world.

*S*urely, Western civilization owes the tube's inventor a big wet kiss, but the origin of this classic is as faded as an unretouched mouth. It was probably introduced around the same time as the eyebrow pencil, circa 1915. Back then, the color stick was moved up and down by a simple slide mechanism rather than a winder, and had a rounded end rather than the point or wedge shape usual today. But the fundamental idea differed little from this state-of-the-art design introduced more recently by the gloss leaders at Estée Lauder. The lines of this hip stick are nothing short of noble, paying more than mere lip service to the current born-again ornamentalism of office-building architecture. Watch for it on a skyline near you.